FUN
GAMES
FOR
GREAT
PARTIES

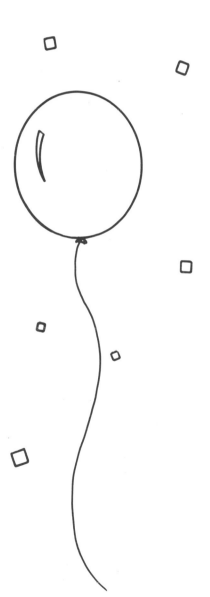

FUN
GAMES
FOR
GREAT
PARTIES

by
Maralys Wills

PRICE STERN SLOAN
Los Angeles

To Madiline
Have fun!
Maralys

"Notorious Numbers" is based on a puzzle which originally appeared in GAMES
MAGAZINE.
"Duck Soup" is by Dan Carlinsky, © Carlinsky Features, and is reprinted by
permission.
ISBN 0-89586-750-8

Cover and interior design: Wilson Design Group
Cover Photography: Anthony Nex Photography

10 9 8 7 6 5 4 3 2

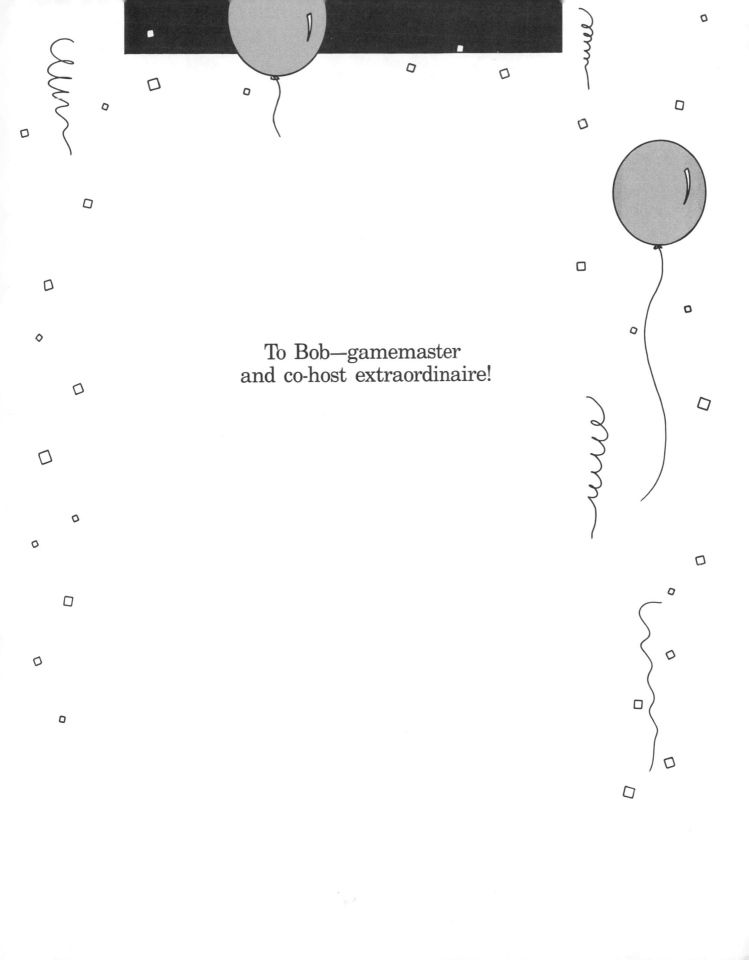

To Bob—gamemaster
and co-host extraordinaire!

TABLE OF CONTENTS

PREFACE

It's a very different word in parties today! People aren't drinking as much. Small talk isn't making it as entertainment. Food isn't the crowning touch, because everyone's dieting.

So what are we to do?

Play games, that's what. Entertain ourselves the way we used to—by being clever, imaginative, funny, smart, competitive, thoughtful, profound.

Which isn't as difficult as it sounds, because that's what the right games can do for us, any of us—make us seem clever, imaginative, funny. . . .

As a host you needn't worry that your party games will fall flat. As long as games are introduced at the beginning (and provided nobody is drunk) you will find that your bright, imaginative guests will get into the spirit and your party will soar.

It happens. Every time.

I am so convinced of this—it's worked for us on so many occasions—that I hereby throw out a challenge: Give me any group of reasonably intelligent, reasonably sober adults and I'll throw a party that will take off like magic.

Twenty-five years ago my husband and I got into games informally and accidentally. We gave a few parties that were lively, guests told others and incredibly soon we were organizing parties all over town—for charities, churches, Little League, the tennis club and of course for ourselves. Guests always went away laughing, which we supposed was the point of it all.

It went on that way for years—people telling us, "We'll bring the food and you plan the games," but we never considered ourselves professionals until our teenaged children roped us into planning *their* parties. That, as anyone knows, meant we'd "arrived."

Herewith we offer what we've learned about *making parties fun.*

INTRODUCTION

The theory behind giving a good party is to structure it so the guests will entertain *each other.* People are quirky, deep, gifted and full of surprises. But the normal party allows only a tiny bit of this to show. At most events you get to know only the guests with the loudest voices, or those who happened to get trapped in the same corner you did.

A well-planned party gives the guests something concrete to *do*—and allows everyone to see everyone else doing it. Along the way, interesting traits come to the surface like cream. Give a great party and your guests will go home knowing who has the rapier wit, who retains information like a computer, who is full of original ideas that bubble forth like hidden springs.

An interesting party can combine diverse ages as easily as mixed nuts. At our latest party the youngest was six and the oldest sixty-six. It didn't matter. It worked beautifully.

Throughout the book we've inserted tips and cautions that can make all the difference in whether a game "works" or not. We've had enough experience in the dynamics of running party games (which is really understanding group psychology) to know that games can soar if done right or stumble if certain details are overlooked.

So trust us. Read the observations that go with each game. Pay attention to such things as fitting games to the size of your crowd. (Games that work well with a dozen people, for instance, could be a disaster with fifty.)

But mainly relax and enjoy the fallout. Let your guests provide the spark. Be a "guest" yourself.

Playing party games is the best way we know to mine the hidden veins of gold among friends and strangers alike. Given a chance, most people are fun. We can attest to it: they've been entertaining us at our parties for twenty-five years.

CHAPTER 1

MIXERS AND STARTERS

Mixers are important because they set the tone for your whole party. It takes more courage than anyone ought to have to propose "games" after the party is in full swing. How many of us have seen a hostess throw cold water on the frivolities and found the group turning mutinous because she suggested charades at the wrong moment?

Charades, in fact, has given party games a bad name.

Yet, the best parties we've been to, and given, usually involved games that were carefully chosen and introduced right at the beginning.

Guests who arrive at the door to find a hat, a pencil or some other prop thrust into their hands immediately become involved. They have a mission. Something is required of them. They are drawn in. Greet them with some kind of task and their expectations are set for the rest of the evening. They are yours and the party is on its way.

There are all sorts of ways to start a party off right. One of the best, we've discovered, is to present your guests with a variety of hats. Over the years we've accumulated nearly a hundred, from pith helmets to black bowlers. We let our guests choose their own, and you have only to see the Superior Court Judge wearing a pink-feathered garden hat to know you're going to have a good time. Beyond that, hats identify hidden yearnings or reveal subliminal bravado. In my wildest imaginings I wouldn't have figured our shy, teenage boy would put on a Phyllis Diller fright wig.

Shoe removal can help set an informal tone. For one afternoon party we put our guests in paper hospital slippers and sent them outdoors. We hadn't anticipated the difficulty they'd have climbing our grassy slope in those paper slippers. Nobody could keep them on. But what a windfall! While newcomers struggled up the incline

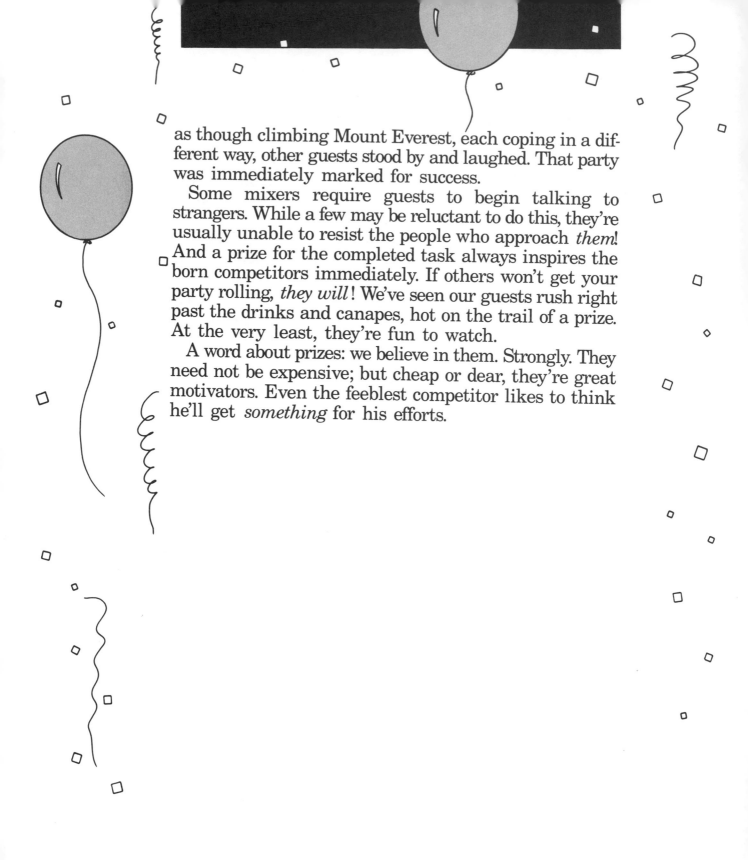

as though climbing Mount Everest, each coping in a different way, other guests stood by and laughed. That party was immediately marked for success.

Some mixers require guests to begin talking to strangers. While a few may be reluctant to do this, they're usually unable to resist the people who approach *them*! And a prize for the completed task always inspires the born competitors immediately. If others won't get your party rolling, *they will*! We've seen our guests rush right past the drinks and canapes, hot on the trail of a prize. At the very least, they're fun to watch.

A word about prizes: we believe in them. Strongly. They need not be expensive; but cheap or dear, they're great motivators. Even the feeblest competitor likes to think he'll get *something* for his efforts.

CAMOUFLAGE

5-30 players

Props: 20-25 small objects, such as safety pin, paper clip, brown thumbtack, red thumbtack, hand-out sheets, pencils
Prize or prizes

Camouflage involves a search for small objects hidden in plain sight in your living room. The interesting thing about this game is how completely an incongruous object can disappear when cleverly placed on a piece of furniture or knicknack of the same color. It is always a fresh surprise to a participant to discover an odd item "right under his nose."

A postage stamp can be glued to the face of a picture. A brown shoelace wound around the leg of a brown chair. A red thumbtack poked into a red design on a sofa pillow. A hairpin laid on a black lamp base. A paper clip hung from a metal light fixture.

Every living room affords endless places to "hide" small objects, and the host can feel incredibly smug about finding that clever, perfect spot. Likewise, the ingenuity of your guests, from the Sherlock Holmes type who stalks his evidence with a gimlet eye, to the pragmatist who stalks the stalker, keeps this game interesting for host and guests alike.

It is important to emphasize to guests that none of the objects are *under* anything and that nothing need be moved as they search. Every object will be in plain sight.

Also, guests should be warned not to touch the objects or give their locations away.

At the end it is important to collect all the guests and let your winner point out where he found everything—thereby enhancing the sense of triumph.

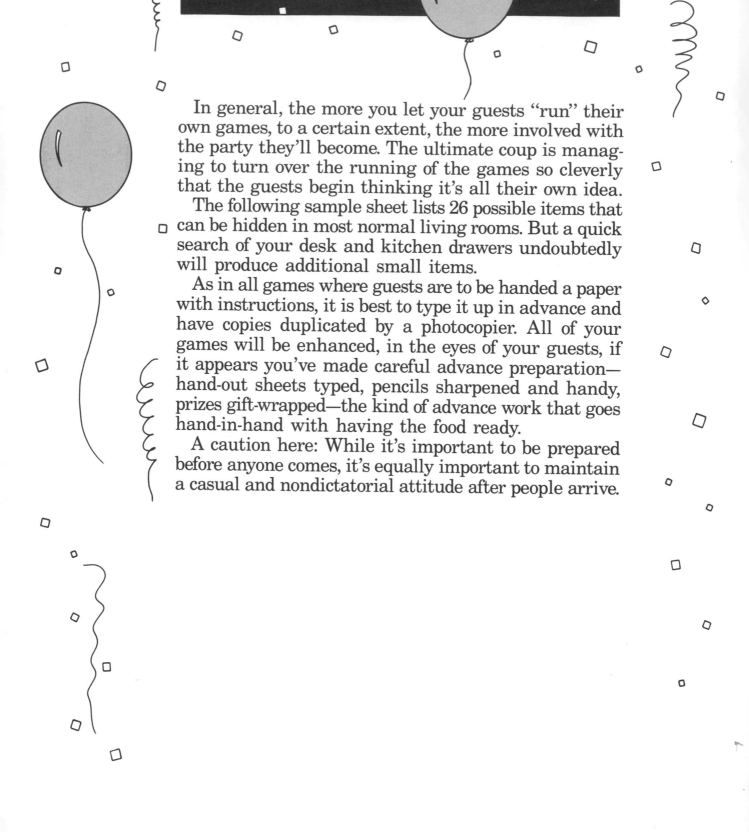

In general, the more you let your guests "run" their own games, to a certain extent, the more involved with the party they'll become. The ultimate coup is managing to turn over the running of the games so cleverly that the guests begin thinking it's all their own idea.

The following sample sheet lists 26 possible items that can be hidden in most normal living rooms. But a quick search of your desk and kitchen drawers undoubtedly will produce additional small items.

As in all games where guests are to be handed a paper with instructions, it is best to type it up in advance and have copies duplicated by a photocopier. All of your games will be enhanced, in the eyes of your guests, if it appears you've made careful advance preparation—hand-out sheets typed, pencils sharpened and handy, prizes gift-wrapped—the kind of advance work that goes hand-in-hand with having the food ready.

A caution here: While it's important to be prepared before anyone comes, it's equally important to maintain a casual and nondictatorial attitude after people arrive.

CAMOUFLAGE

Directions:

You may begin looking for the items listed below. They are all to be found in the living room, and all are in plain sight. You won't have to move anything to find them. They will all be in incongruous places (no matches in ashtrays, etc.) but well camouflaged. When you find an item, leave it where it is and play it cool—why help anyone else? There is a prize for the first person finding everything on the list.

Item	**Where Found**
1. Penny	
2. Burnt Match	
3. White Button	
4. Bobby Pin	
5. Paper Clip	
6. Bathroom Key	
7. Aspirin	
8. Toothpick	
9. Brown Shoestring	
10. Red Thumbtack	
11. Silver Earring	
12. Red Twine	

13. Pink Tube of Lipstick   _____

14. Safety Pin   _____

15. Emery Board   _____

16. Rubber Band   _____

17. White Thimble   _____

18. Vitamin Capsule   _____

19. Prune Pit   _____

20. Milk Bottle Top   _____

21. Postage Stamp   _____

22. Silver Belt Buckle   _____

23. Tea Bag   _____

24. Green Clothespin   _____

25. Small Light Bulb   _____

26. Red Ladybug   _____

AMNESIA

5-50 players

Props: name tags with names of famous people, instruction sheets or poster with printed rules

As the guests come in the door, the host greets them by pinning name tags on their backs. It is then explained, via instruction sheets or a poster, that the guest has amnesia and is to find out who he or she is by asking questions of the other guests. Each guest is allowed to ask only two questions of any one person, and each question must be answered with a simple yes or no.

The point of limiting the questions is to force people to circulate.

The game ends when most people have figured out who they are. If the host wishes to add incentive, he or she can offer to open the bar only when each individual guest is able to identify him or herself. (It is probably becoming obvious how steadfastly we lean toward incentives!)

THE HAT-MIXER

10-50 players

Props: A variety of hats, at least one for each person present, and preferably more (the more varied and numerous the hats, the better the game)
Prizes

Though we've been using hats in an unstructured way for years, we discovered recently that hats can serve as more than mood setters. With a little planning, they become the basis for a mixer that may last all evening.

The beauty of this game is that it contains two or three surprises for your guests, plus ongoing amusement which lasts even after guests know what's coming. The game starts innocently enough, when arriving guests are asked to choose a hat from among a large collection. (Hats have always found high acceptance at our parties, even though we've repeated the gimmick periodically over the years. Try leaving them out and someone will always ask, "Hey, where are the hats?")

The wrinkle is that a few of the hats are marked inside, and the marking is known only to the hosts. At our recent Caribbean party we used two kinds of price stickers, but anything will do—a red thread, a safety pin, an inked dot.

At some point after the party is under way, the host rings a bell or sounds a gong and announces loudly, "Everybody switch hats!" This creates momentary surprise; after all, guests have carefully chosen the hat which is *them,* and now they're being asked to switch. But after that flicker of hesitation they switch and new layers of merriment are added to the party: the round-faced fellow, for instance, may look a lot funnier in the pith helmet than he did in the black beret.

At intervals throughout the party, guests are told to make additional switches, maybe three, until finally the host announces that all must take off their hats and look inside. "If there's a little round sticker there, you get a prize." It's probably best if the prize is something nice; that way it seems like such an unexpected windfall.

The mixer can continue with another, different set of markings and a second set of prizes given later.

For us, this mixer was such a success that the party was spirited from beginning to end. Switching hats meant a passing parade of new personas and lent an intimacy that could not have been achieved any other way. The visual impact of all those crazy hats, some suitable, some outrageous, was its own reward.

How can anyone be stiff, pompous or stuffy when wearing a toreador's hat?

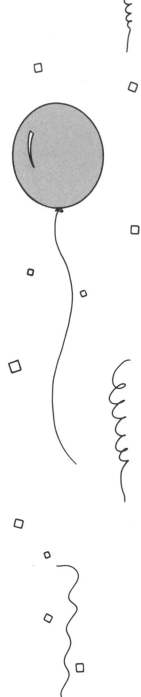

EXPOSES

5-30 players

Props: hand-out sheets (see sample), pencils
Prize or prizes

This unusual icebreaker takes some advance preparation, but is always worth the effort because the guests seem to enjoy it so much. Party goers must be called in advance and asked to reveal some interesting, little-known fact about themselves—something they are proud of, or something odd or funny—and always a bit of information most of the other guests won't know already. For instance, did he win some honor in high school or college, did she meet a celebrity under strange circumstances, receive some accolade or funny reprimand or cause some hilarious mishap or survive some kind of hair-raising experience? The possibilities are endless. In everyone's background there is *something*.

The facts are then typed out on a single sheet with blanks to be filled in. Guests are given the sheets and a pencil as they come in the door and asked to identify which fact belongs to which person. A prize goes to the first person who completes the sheet.

The outstanding feature of this game is that guests are already involved in the party before they get there. We've never found anyone who wasn't pleased to offer some interesting tidbit about his or her life. Furthermore, almost everyone rises to the task of discovering the odd and interesting facts about others.

After somebody has won the game, we always gather our guests into a circle and go over the list in greater detail, letting the guests identify themselves and expand on their unusual experiences. Invariably this becomes the highlight of the evening as one by one each person relives an interesting moment. Everyone leaves knowing everyone else a little better . . . and it really is fun to learn that an old friend actually beat Dinah Shore on her own tennis court, was a spelunker in Arkansas, set his beard on fire or fell on her face in front of John Barrymore.

The following sample sheet is a compilation of experiences from our own guests.

Directions:

Fill in names in your own hand. Find someone who . . .

1. Has sung in several European countries
2. Broke the escalator at Macy's
3. Is a graduate engineer who flunked Heat Transfer
4. Won a regional spelling bee in Indiana
5. Was offered a major studio screen test
6. Taught handicapped children to ski
7. Played trumpet in the Stanford band
8. Has her autograph on your dollar bill
9. Was 4th of July queen in Yorkville, Illinois
10. "Practices" the piano in bed
11. Was a spelunker in Arkansas
12. Bought black market rubles in Russia
13. Was kicked out of Sunday School, age 3
14. Fell on her face in front of John Barrymore
15. Had five accidents in the same car
16. Hands out thousands of dollars a day
17. Killed a bear at age 12
18. Rode a motorcycle from Riverside to Nova Scotia
19. Flunked a Ceramics course
20. Was carried out to sea in a riptide
21. Was hit in the nose with an angry rake
22. Held a county swim record for five years

TIDBITS

15-50 players

Props: hand-out sheets (see sample), pencils
Prize or prizes

Though *Tidbits* is similar to *Exposes*, it is an easier mixer to prepare because the questions are general instead of specific, and no one need be called ahead of time. This game is particularly useful for a large crowd.

Guests are handed the sheet and a pencil as they come in the door. The object is to locate appropriate people and fill in the squares with as many names as possible, a prize going to the person who collects the most names. It's a mixer which starts people talking to one another at the slow beginning of a party, and is particularly good to use among strangers.

The following sample sheet can be modified in a variety of ways—from making the questions thematic, to making them funnier, more personal, more exotic or more pointed. A Washington, D.C. hostess, for instance, might opt for categories having to do with politics.

Directions: *Have as many qualified persons as you can find sign in the proper squares. There will be a prize for the sheet with the most correct names.*

Has a hundred dollars in his pocket	Has worn braces	Is wearing contact lenses
Has a traffic ticket in her purse	Was born in the same state you were	Has pierced ears
Is carrying old movie stubs	Is wearing red socks	Has a fifty dollar bill
Has red hair	Will admit she's past forty-five	Is carrying a pocket watch
Has an appendicitis scar	Has a Southern accent	Has 5 or more children

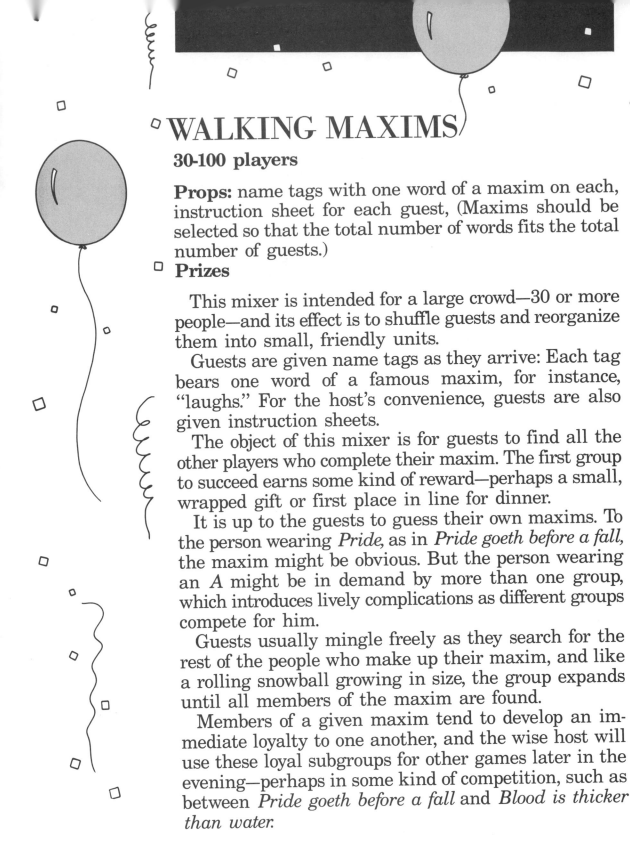

WALKING MAXIMS

30-100 players

Props: name tags with one word of a maxim on each, instruction sheet for each guest, (Maxims should be selected so that the total number of words fits the total number of guests.)

Prizes

This mixer is intended for a large crowd—30 or more people—and its effect is to shuffle guests and reorganize them into small, friendly units.

Guests are given name tags as they arrive: Each tag bears one word of a famous maxim, for instance, "laughs." For the host's convenience, guests are also given instruction sheets.

The object of this mixer is for guests to find all the other players who complete their maxim. The first group to succeed earns some kind of reward—perhaps a small, wrapped gift or first place in line for dinner.

It is up to the guests to guess their own maxims. To the person wearing *Pride,* as in *Pride goeth before a fall,* the maxim might be obvious. But the person wearing an *A* might be in demand by more than one group, which introduces lively complications as different groups compete for him.

Guests usually mingle freely as they search for the rest of the people who make up their maxim, and like a rolling snowball growing in size, the group expands until all members of the maxim are found.

Members of a given maxim tend to develop an immediate loyalty to one another, and the wise host will use these loyal subgroups for other games later in the evening—perhaps in some kind of competition, such as between *Pride goeth before a fall* and *Blood is thicker than water.*

Instructions: *In one corner of your name tag is a word. This word is one of (6) words making up a well-known, timeworn maxim or expression— for example,* Rome wasn't built in a day. *Find the other 5 people carrying the words necessary to complete your aphorism—look for key words and test your word with them—then come to us as a group for verification. The first two complete groups will receive prizes.*

Maxims—Five Words

Blood is thicker than water.
Pride goeth before a fall.
Handsome is as handsome does.
Virtue is its own reward.
Beauty is only skin deep.
Actions speak louder than words.

Maxims—Six Words

Great oaks from little acorns
   grow.
He who laughs last laughs best.
A stitch in time saves nine.
If the shoe fits, wear it.
God helps those who help
   themselves.
A rolling stone gathers no moss.
Brevity is the soul of wit.
Absence makes the heart grow
   fonder.
Home is where the heart is.
Rome wasn't built in a day.
A kite flies against the wind.
There is no substitute for victory.
Damn the torpedoes, full speed
   ahead.
All that glitters is not gold.
Living well is the best revenge.

Maxims—Seven Words

The pen is mightier than the
   sword.
Don't count your chickens before
   they hatch.
Eternal vigilance is the price of
   liberty.
Money is the root of all evil.
The hand is quicker than the eye.
A penny saved is a penny earned.
To err is human, to forgive divine.
All is fair in love and war.

BODY SEARCH

10-40 players

Props: ten small items, such as an emery board, a small key, a tiny gold safety pin, a piece of white string, instruction sheets
Prize or prizes

Similar to *Camouflage,* this game calls for items to be hidden on *people* instead of in the living room.

Each of the first ten arrivals is taken aside by the host, who "conceals" one of the small objects on the guest's person—in plain view, of course. A paper clip, for instance, can be worn as an earring, a small gold safety pin added to a belt buckle, someone's brown shoe given a white shoestring, a tiny key worn as a lapel ornament. Once again, the main idea is that the object be in plain sight, well camouflaged and entirely incongruous.

Subsequent guests are given instruction sheets which list the items and leave blanks for recording who is wearing what. A prize goes to the first guest whose search enables him or her to fill in all the blanks with correct names.

The game is inclined to inspire a certain amount of friendly and suggestive scrutiny . . . and who minds?

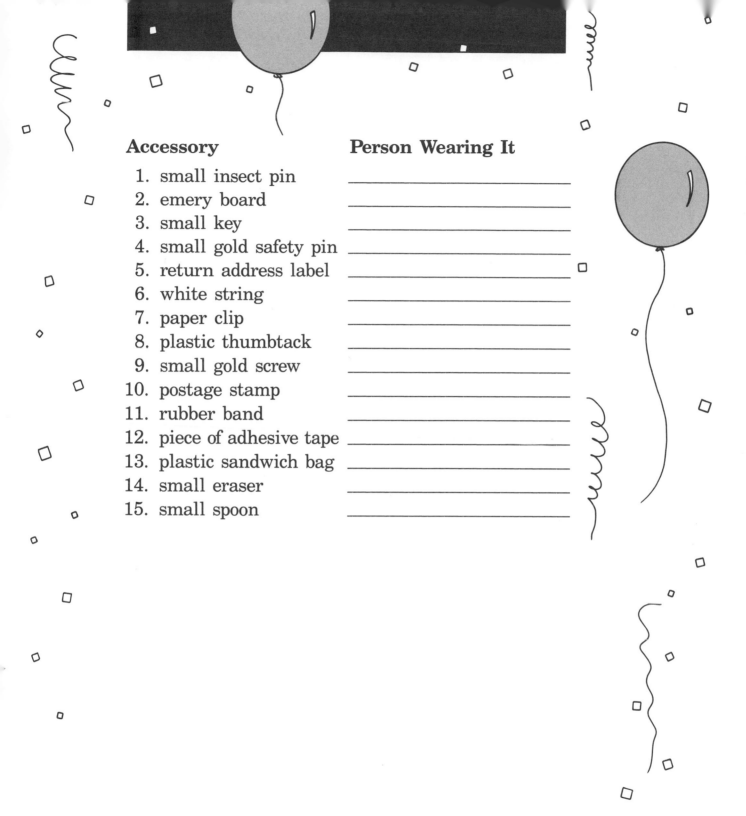

Accessory	Person Wearing It
1. small insect pin	_____
2. emery board	_____
3. small key	_____
4. small gold safety pin	_____
5. return address label	_____
6. white string	_____
7. paper clip	_____
8. plastic thumbtack	_____
9. small gold screw	_____
10. postage stamp	_____
11. rubber band	_____
12. piece of adhesive tape	_____
13. plastic sandwich bag	_____
14. small eraser	_____
15. small spoon	_____

ANTHONY AND CLEOPATRA

10-40 players

Props: name tags with scrambled names of famous pairs (see list)

The idea of this mixer is to pair up arriving men and women into new couples with such illustrious names as Franklin and Eleanor.

Women are given name tags with scrambled letters representing a noted woman, while men wear the scrambled name of some famous man. But all are members of well-known pair: Hamlet and Ophelia, Albert and Victoria, Napoleon and Josephine. The possibilities are endless and the host should consider updating the list with current, noteworthy personalities.

Guest are given their mystery name tags as they arrive and are told that they must find their opposite halves as quickly as possible. While most guests will participate readily, the host can add additional incentives to ensure cooperation—such as place cards at the table which indicate Anthony and Cleopatra will be a couple at dinner or later games, in which couples will compete as a team.

This is a mixer which discourages that familiar scenario where all the men gather in one part of the room and the women in another.

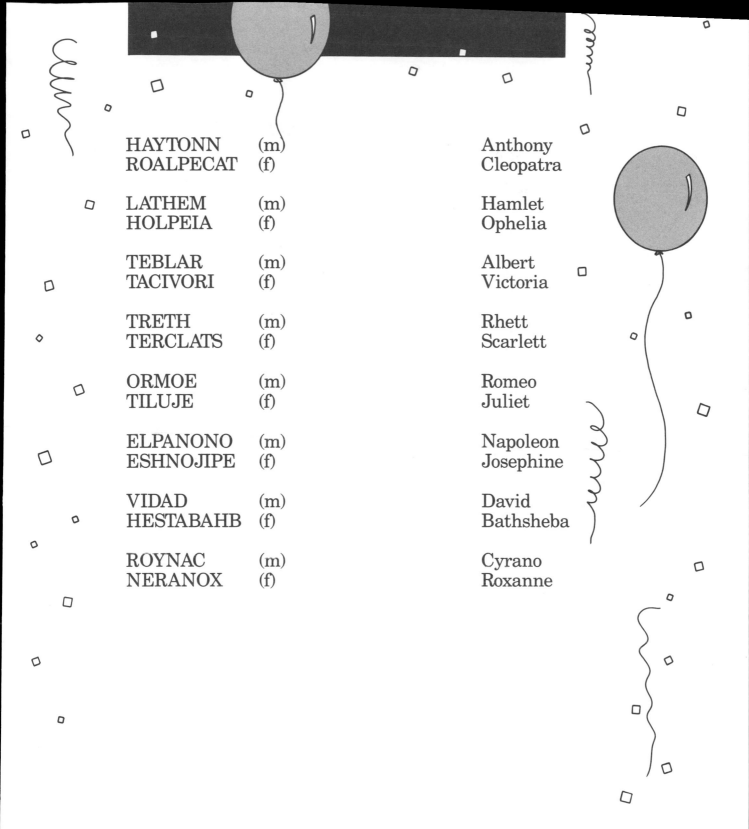

HAYTONN	(m)	Anthony
ROALPECAT	(f)	Cleopatra
LATHEM	(m)	Hamlet
HOLPEIA	(f)	Ophelia
TEBLAR	(m)	Albert
TACIVORI	(f)	Victoria
TRETH	(m)	Rhett
TERCLATS	(f)	Scarlett
ORMOE	(m)	Romeo
TILUJE	(f)	Juliet
ELPANONO	(m)	Napoleon
ESHNOJIPE	(f)	Josephine
VIDAD	(m)	David
HESTABAHB	(f)	Bathsheba
ROYNAC	(m)	Cyrano
NERANOX	(f)	Roxanne

PIRATE TREASURE HUNT

10-28 players

Props: "Pirate Treasure Hunt" sheets (one per team), one or two scrambled "clue words" written on small pieces of paper
Prizes

The object of this mixer is to find the hidden clues and decipher the scrambled words that make up the phrase, "Pieces of eight and gold doubloons—Long John Silver's Treasure." It becomes a mixer when guests are assigned to teams (with people they may not know well) and given the task of coming up with the phrase.

Each team (of 2-to-4 people) is given a Pirate Treasure Hunt sheet and assigned to begin its treasure hunt in one of a number of different locales around the house or grounds. The purpose of starting in different places is to avoid congestion.

The sheet lists various cryptic sentences which describe the location of the scrambled words. Teams search for the scrambled words, then pause to try to unscramble them before proceeding to the next station. A gong or bell stops the search in one room and sends the team to the next.

Plenty of good-natured confusion results when teams rush past each other switching to new locations.

At the end, the team that figures out the phrase first wins a prize—and it should be a good one after all that work!

Seven "clues" are hidden in the following places: living room, family room, den, dining room, kitchen, patio, front porch.

Go to the places in the order given. You'll have ten minutes to find the clue and unscramble the word. If the gong rings and you haven't found it or unscrambled it, move on to the next place. You can go back and finish after the last clue. Be very careful not to reveal the location of the clue to another group—you don't want to help them win! All clues are visible—none are under or inside anything.

When you have all the clue words unscrambled, put them together to form a pirate phrase. First team that gets it right wins the Pirates' Treasure!

Team #	Place	Mystery Location
____	**Patio**	5 paces north of 8 bells (near wind chimes)
____	**Living room**	This is handy for finding treasure or burying mates (fireplace shovel)
____	**Kitchen**	Shiver me timbers, it's cold (refrigerator)
____	**Dining room**	Southeast of Greenwich time and below the flickering flame (near a clock and candle)
____	**Den**	Tales of mutiny curl these pages (on book, "Mutiny on the Bounty")
____	**Family room**	Oh, bright the light throughout the night (on the chandelier)
____	**Front porch**	10 paces west of impatiens, 4 paces still to climb (near pot of impatiens beyond steps)

TRUE OR FALSE

5-30 players

Props: blank papers, pencils

In our years of giving parties, this has proven to be one of the best-received and certainly the easiest in our collection of get-acquainted games. We've played it on the spur of the moment on all kinds of informal occasions and it's *always* a hit. It's a do-anywhere game because no preparation is needed.

Guests are handed blank sheets and pencils and asked to write down two true statements about themselves and one false, in any order they choose.

Later, the group convenes and one by one guests read their statements—after each the group guesses which item is false.

We played this game recently in a group where few people knew each other. It became a fast and fascinating way to get acquainted. Was that slightly overweight man really a skier? Did the conservative fellow in a business suit race motorcycles? (He did!) Was the mother of four children a former ballet dancer? (She was!) Did that grinning young man once date a Miss America contestant? (He didn't!)

Your guests will surprise you every time!

NO-NO NAME TAGS
10-50 players

Props: name tags for each guest
Prize

This rather tricky little mixer appeals to the naturally acquisitive. The purpose is to "win" the name tags of other guests, with a prize going to the person who collects the most.

The method is simple: One guest asks another a question, and if the guest being asked can be tricked into answering "No," the questioner gets his or her name tag. The trick is to think of questions which are naturally answered in the negative. It takes a clever and purposeful guest!

At a recent party, one girl we know managed to collect name tags from nearly every person in the room. She may or may not have gotten a prize; all we heard was what a good time she had.

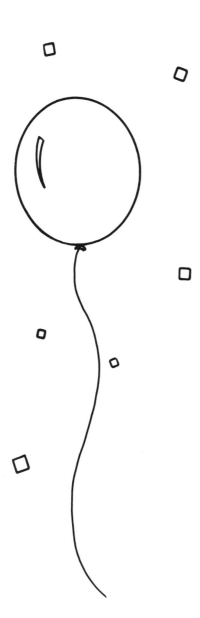

CHAPTER 2

PSYCHOLOGICAL/ PHILOSOPHICAL GAMES

Psychological/Philosophical games are unique in that there are no right or wrong answers and no winners. Yet even without the element of competition, guests find these games highly entertaining and full of surprises. Most either illuminate human nature—which, of course, is never consistent and seldom dull—or give the guests a chance to examine their own values. Answers often come as a revelation, even to spouses.

This might be the time for a caution about games in general. It is a temptation for any host captivated by games to plan too many for a given party and then, as she sees the evening slipping away, to frantically urge her guests to play every one.

A mistake.

First and foremost, the good host is relaxed and casual. If one of the games takes longer than planned; so be it. Guests like to linger over events they enjoy. If time gets away between games, that's all right, too. People can't be regimented every minute.

For a long party, such as one on New Year's eve, we generally plan four or five games. But it usually works out that we play only three. In between, people want to chat, eat and drink. Let them. We don't want people thinking they're back in grammar school.

Playing games successfully is always a matter both of spotting the lulls and being ready with a new activity—and also keeping one's antennae out, sensing any shift in the mood of the crowd. People don't mind being herded a little, but there's a thin line between a little and too much.

You will know it's been a good party when somebody looks at a clock and says in astonishment, "I can't believe it got so late!"

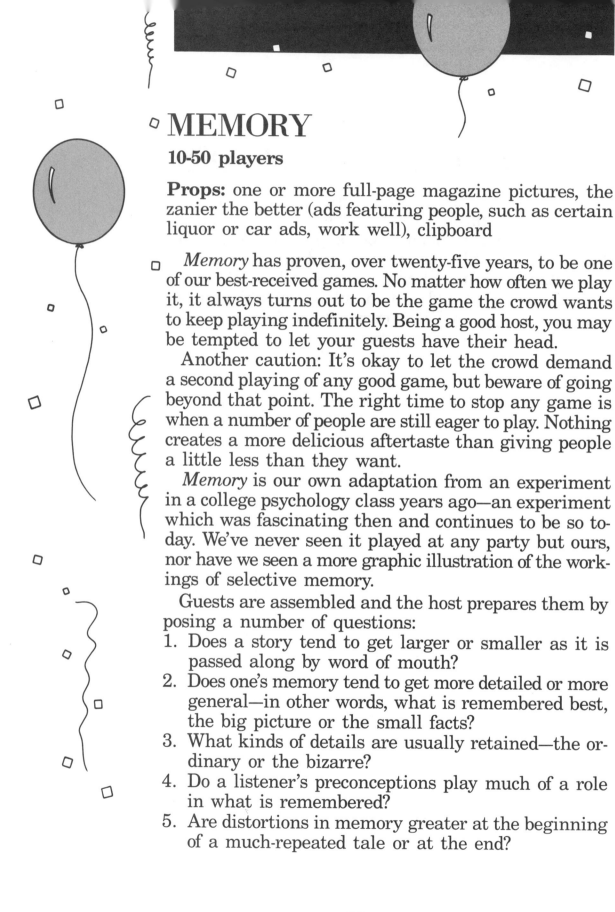

MEMORY

10-50 players

Props: one or more full-page magazine pictures, the zanier the better (ads featuring people, such as certain liquor or car ads, work well), clipboard

Memory has proven, over twenty-five years, to be one of our best-received games. No matter how often we play it, it always turns out to be the game the crowd wants to keep playing indefinitely. Being a good host, you may be tempted to let your guests have their head.

Another caution: It's okay to let the crowd demand a second playing of any good game, but beware of going beyond that point. The right time to stop any game is when a number of people are still eager to play. Nothing creates a more delicious aftertaste than giving people a little less than they want.

Memory is our own adaptation from an experiment in a college psychology class years ago—an experiment which was fascinating then and continues to be so today. We've never seen it played at any party but ours, nor have we seen a more graphic illustration of the workings of selective memory.

Guests are assembled and the host prepares them by posing a number of questions:
1. Does a story tend to get larger or smaller as it is passed along by word of mouth?
2. Does one's memory tend to get more detailed or more general—in other words, what is remembered best, the big picture or the small facts?
3. What kinds of details are usually retained—the ordinary or the bizarre?
4. Do a listener's preconceptions play much of a role in what is remembered?
5. Are distortions in memory greater at the beginning of a much-repeated tale or at the end?

The guests will probably call out opinions, and sometimes the host will want to take a vote, but be careful not to reveal answers.

Thus prepared, five or six people are sent out of the room. The host then brings out a picture on a clipboard and props it on a chair for everyone to see. (The more unusual the picture, the better the game; bizarre details help make the point.) Once everyone has examined the picture, one of the players is brought back and stands behind the chair, where the clipboard can't be seen. The host (or another guest) then describes the picture carefully, starting with an overview and progressing to the smallest details, being careful to say everything only once.

The first player then calls back a second, and in front of everyone, (with the picture still visible only to the crowd) relates all he can remember of the host's description of the scene. Once finished, the first player is allowed to see the picture—which is always a revelation and usually amusing to the crowd.

The second player, in turn, calls for a third and tells the story in the same manner and the game continues until the last player repeats the remembered story to the whole group.

The audience, able to see the picture throughout, is invariably surprised to witness an ever-changing fabric of misinformation, lost details and made-up facts.

It may come as a surprise, even to the host, to learn that stories shrink instead of growing larger, that the more bizarre the elements, the quicker forgotten and that each retelling results in a predictable loss of facts. Furthermore, distortion seems to progress at an ever faster rate.

WISHES AND WON'TS

5-30 players

Props: papers and pencils

The host assigns a number to each guest, who then write the number, but no name, on a piece of paper. Players are asked to write down three secret ambitions, such as, "I've always wanted to fly a hang glider." "I've dreamed of starring opposite Robert Redford." "I've always wanted to climb Kilimanjaro."

Next they're asked to list three things they'd never do: "I'd never wear a rented bathing suit." "I'd never drive a school bus." "I'd never listen to jazz."

Good examples from the host are helpful to fire guests' imaginations.

At the end of 10 minutes papers are collected and redistributed. Guests write down everyone's number and who they think that person is as the players in turn read the lists they've been given. The player who guesses the greatest number of people correctly wins.

The game works best if players are cautioned to be honest about their wishes and won'ts—imaginative but honest. It's interesting how often husbands and wives will fail to identify each other, "I never knew you cared about hang gliders!"

HEAVEN AND HELL

10-30 players

Props: papers and pencils

After guests are given paper and pencil, the host asks them to list 5 definitions of heaven, 5 definitions of hell.

One recent list, for instance, defined heaven as consisting of brooks, forests, harmonious music, college courses and round table discussions. Hell was radio commercials, lines of people for everything, a cigarette butt and trash strewn landscape and having to live with the American teenage mentality.

After fifteen minutes, papers are gathered and redistributed for reading aloud. Guests try to guess who gave which definitions, a denouement which proves to be intrinsically interesting. (Is there anyone else out there who feels hell would be a room full of crying babies for whom nobody can do anything?)

PURE AT HEART

5-30 players

Props: the *Pure at Heart* Story (4 or 5 copies for a large group), papers and pencils

The following story raises interesting moral questions which are complex enough to engender long and thoughtful discussion.

For smaller groups, the host reads the story aloud and individuals make their own judgments.

But the game is more interesting when played by larger numbers, in which case the group is divided into several smaller units (5-7 people each) which are sent to separate rooms to make a joint decision.

When the groups are brought back, answers are compared and reasons given—which usually prompts even more discussion. It has been our experience that groups seldom agree on their answers, and that each is able to muster strong arguments in support of its decisions.

A ship was lost at sea. Six survivors made their way to two small islands separated by shark-infested waters. Pearl was a damsel fair, engaged to marry John.

The two were separated in the disaster, finding themselves on different islands. Pearl was stranded with Tom, Dick and Harry, while John was on the other island with Roger.

Pearl spotted John across the channel, but she also saw the sharks in the water. She approached Tom with a request that he help her construct a raft to cross the channel. But Tom said he was too busy building a larger boat which could carry all the survivors to safety.

Pearl then asked Dick to help her with a raft, which Dick said he'd do—provided she slept with him first.

Pearl refused and approached Harry, who told her he had plenty to worry about besides reuniting her with her fiance, and besides, he didn't want to get involved.

Pearl waited two days to see if John would be able to devise some means of crossing the channel to reach her, but there was no vegetation or driftwood on John's island.

Pearl finally decided to meet Dick's terms, and the morning after her surrender, Dick devised a driftwood raft and took Pearl across to John.

When Pearl reached John and John learned of Pearl's compromise with Dick, he spurned her.

Roger, observing Pearl's distress and learning of her course of action, offered to marry Pearl himself.

Rank these six people in order of their moral or ethical strength—from most noble or admirable to most despicable.

There are no right or wrong answers.

BARE ESSENTIALS

10-30 players

Props: papers and pencils

This is another philosophical game the purpose of which is to inspire thoughtful discussion about aspects of civilization we take for granted.

Guests are told they will be asked to evaluate the importance of various inventions since the discovery of fire. The question is, which five inventions could you least live without? Guests are divided into three groups and each group is sent to a different room. One member of each group will be asked to list the group's consensus, in descending order of importance. For example, we could least live without the printing press.

Players may consider such items as the printing press, radio, telephone, electric light bulb, automobile, television, steam engine, airplane, refrigerator, medical inventions, even the wheel. The host should not enumerate all the possibilities, but rather let the guests recall various inventions for themselves. Players will probably find, to their surprise, that they've overlooked some major inventions.

The denouement comes when, after about twenty minutes, guests are called back into the room and the three lists are compared. It is our experience that no two lists will look even remotely alike, and that guests will want to go on debating the relative importance of their choices.

The perceptive host will try to discontinue the discussion while guests still find it interesting.

LISTENING

5-10 players

Props: papers and pencils

This game is best played by a small crowd who know each other well. Five to 10 participants are best.

The host introduces the game by asking the group how well they really listen to others: "Do you really pay attention to what other people say? Do you have an ear for the speech patterns of your friends?"

The host then gives each person one slip of paper for every other person in the room. So, with 10 guests present, each person receives 9 slips of paper.

Players are asked to label their slips with the names of those present. Then comes the hooker—they are asked to write down the favorite expression, saying or sentence of each of the other guests.

At first there may be resistance to the idea, but people get into this game. A little thought and it becomes fun. What *does* Mary Wilson say all the time?

The host can give suggestions, such as, "It's easiest if you close your eyes and 'listen' to the voices of your friends." The game is working when the host begins to see smiles here and there and guests start writing faster.

At the end of about fifteen minutes, papers are collected and the host sorts all the Mary's into one pile, all the Bob's into another and so on.

Now comes the fun. The host asks, "Who is this?" and without further identification, reads all the statements about Bob. If guests know each other well, it will take only one or two declarations to bring recognition from the group. It is not only amusing for each guest to hear statements about the others, but usually fun to hear your own speech as others hear it. Since people are invariably polite in a company situation, the host need not worry that anyone will get their feelings hurt.

TOP TEN

10-30 players

Props: papers and pencils

Top Ten is a perfect game for New Year's eve.

Papers and pencils are distributed and guests are asked to list, as quickly as they can, the 10 most newsworthy events of the past year. Speed is important; the host wants to know which events come the most quickly to everyone's mind.

After about 10 minutes, players are asked to read their lists aloud. Most people will be surprised to find how many major events they've forgotten—episodes so large they dominated the news for weeks.

This is a satisfying game—a way of reviewing a year and putting it into perspective from the vantage point of the year's end.

FREEDOMS

6-30 players

Props: papers and pencils, one for each group

The host introduces this game by asking the guests to imagine that each of them has been made a political prisoner of a totalitarian country and put into an isolation cell. "All your rights and normal pleasures have been taken away. But, for propaganda reasons, and to show its great mercy, the government has decided to grant you certain rights and privileges, a new one each month. Which would you ask for first?" Guests are told they will be put into groups, and each group must decide its own rankings, from most important privileges to least important.

After three groups are selected by count-off, the host hands out papers and pencils and asks one member of each group to list the following "Rights." (Lists may be made up in advance and a list handed to each group.) This list might include: the freedom to write letters, a choice of foods, the right to bathe and brush one's teeth, the right to speak freely, the right to visit other prisoners, books to read, freedom from brain washing, the right to have one visitor a month. Groups are sent to separate areas to compile their lists.

As in all games where groups must reach a consensus, this game offers insight into the peculiarities of group dynamics. Since different groups will invariably arrive at different rankings, guests will observe that in some instances the group is dominated by a single, strong personality, whereas in others democracy prevails. In a few instances two or three individuals band together to sway the rest.

The end result is not too different from what happens in a jury room.

FOLLOWING ORDERS

10-40 players

Props: instruction sheets (see sample), pencils

Little explanation is needed for this game. Before the host passes out the sheets, everyone is warned that this will be a test of how well they follow instructions. The host says the test will be self-explanatory, but that nobody is to read it until everyone has a copy, and players should be aware there's a time limit.

Sheets are passed out, and on a call of *Go*, players read their instructions.

The fastest readers (and those who really do follow instructions) will get to the end of the test fast and begin to notice that their fellow players really aren't following the rules. Certain directions within the test call for an audible response, and as a few players here and there respond out loud, the game gets funnier and funnier for those paying attention.

This is a game which tends to trap the smartest and quickest.

48

Name: _____

1. Read the sheet before you start working, but *work as fast as you can.*
2. Print your last name in the upper right hand corner of this sheet.
3. Draw a line through the word "corner" in sentence two.
4. Sign your name at the bottom of the sheet.
5. Stop for a second and take a deep breath.
6. Write the city where you were born: _____.
7. Now circle the word "city" in sentence six.
8. Put an "X" in the upper left corner of this sheet.
9. Tear off the corner above the "X."
10. Circle sentence five.
11. Write down your favorite hobby: _____.
12. Speak your first name out loud when you get here.
13. Close your eyes, raise your right arm and wave it.
14. If you think you've been following instructions to here, nod your head.
15. Draw a circle around your birth city.
16. Recite the alphabet from A to G.
17. Circle the numbers all the way down the page.
18. Now that you've finished reading the sheet, go back and do only the second and sixth instructions. Ignore all others, pretend you're writing. Don't let on to the others that they might be doing it wrong. Watch and listen, and you'll see how many people *really* follow instructions.

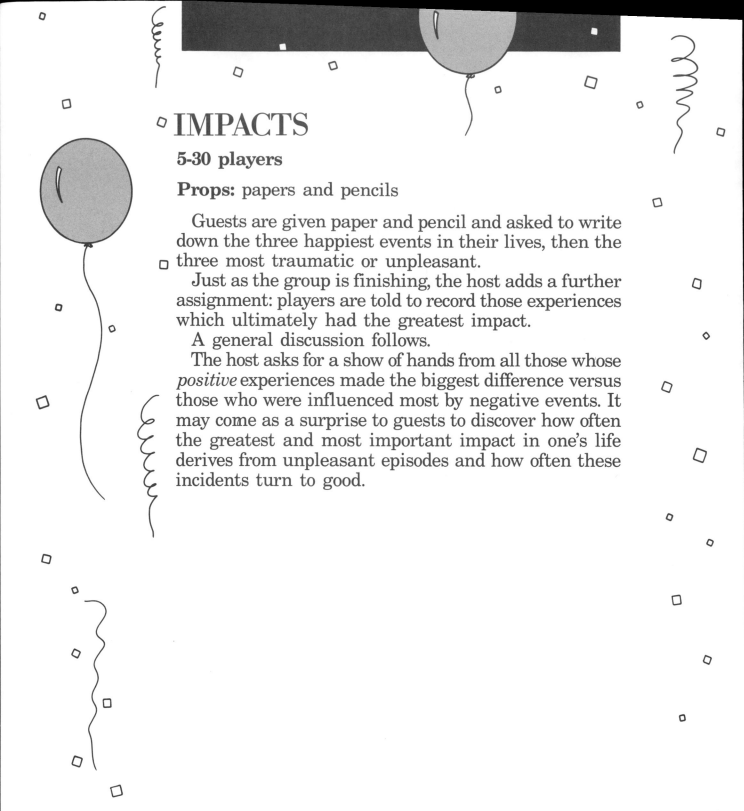

IMPACTS

5-30 players

Props: papers and pencils

Guests are given paper and pencil and asked to write down the three happiest events in their lives, then the three most traumatic or unpleasant.

Just as the group is finishing, the host adds a further assignment: players are told to record those experiences which ultimately had the greatest impact.

A general discussion follows.

The host asks for a show of hands from all those whose *positive* experiences made the biggest difference versus those who were influenced most by negative events. It may come as a surprise to guests to discover how often the greatest and most important impact in one's life derives from unpleasant episodes and how often these incidents turn to good.

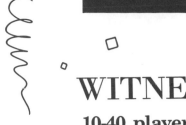

WITNESSES

10-40 players

Props: papers and pencils

The host takes 3 or 4 extroverts aside and asks them to go into another room and make up a 10-second mini-play. The little play can be about anything: a robbery, a murder, an accident or any dramatic event. It must be kept short and vivid.

When the actors report back, the host makes sure everyone is seated before announcing that the group is about to witness an important event, to which they must play close attention. "You will all be witnesses," she says. "Your testimony will be needed."

The actors perform their little scene for the benefit of the others. Then the witnesses are told they have one minute to write down and describe what they saw.

Next the host announces that the "police" have come and witnesses are to read their statements aloud.

One by one, guests fill the air with lies.

At the end it begins to seem that the group must have witnessed a number of different events. As is the case with so many eyewitness accounts, details vary so wildly that everyone's credibility is tarnished.

The game can be played once more. But don't let it go a third round. Keep everyone wishing it had lasted longer.

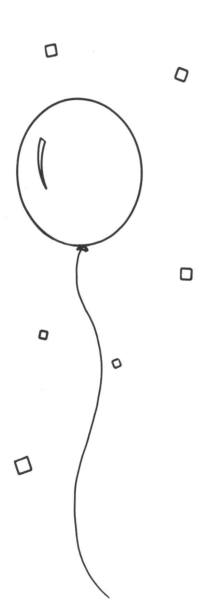

CHAPTER 3

IMAGINATION GAMES

In the finest tradition of parlor games, these games call on the imaginations of the participants to provide the spark. The more originality among your guests, the more fun everyone will have. The greatest pleasure of all lies in discovering that unexpected bit of freshness that resides somewhere in all of us.

DEFINITIONS

8-30 players

Props: a list of obscure words chosen from the dictionary, papers and pencils

The group is divided into two teams which sit across the room from each other. The host passes out blank papers and pencils to everyone, with a warning that nobody is to look at the paper until told to do so. The host then gives each team a different, exotic word from the dictionary, a word that is obviously too obscure to be known by the crowd. Players are now instructed to write the word down—except that one member of each team has already been given the correct definition on his or her paper. (That person must pretend to be writing, too.) Players are instructed to write out their own, imagined definitions of their team's word, with the host pointing out that definitions can be imaginative, humorous or serious. For example, somebody once defined "Troglodyte" as "somebody who troggles."

After a few minutes, the host collects all the definitions for one team, shuffles them and hands them back again. Players take turns reading aloud the definitions they've been given. The opposing team listens and tries to decide which is the correct definition. If they guess correctly they are given one point.

The same procedure is followed for the opposing team. The game is played again with new words and the first team collecting 3 or 5 points wins.

This game is played more for fun than competition. With imaginative guests the game can be truly hilarious.

Here are some sample words we've used: corybantic, rebec, cephalic, buprestid, quiddity.

While the real entertainment in this game invariably results from the zany and frequently funny definitions offered by imaginative guests, it's important to keep up the pretense that "points" and "winning" are the true goals. If the competitive aspect is dropped (as we saw happen recently) guests sense that the host is relying on laughs to make the game work. Suddenly everyone feels a compulsion to chuckle, even when the definitions aren't funny—as they sometimes aren't. There goes your spontaneity and the game becomes a strain.

So keep the competitive aspect going and let the laughs fall where they may.

SHADES AND HUES

5-30 players

Props: papers and pencils

This game is prefaced by the host asking the group whether they've ever thought about the many words used to describe colors, such as red. As a challenge, groups will be asked to see how many variations they can find to describe a single given color.

After guests have been divided into three groups, the host names them the red group, the white group and the blue group. Each group will be assigned its own room or space and given the task of seeing which of the groups, in 10 minutes, can come up with the greatest number of names for a color. Examples would be: watermelon or cherry for red, teal or azure for blue, sand or oatmeal for white.

Color choices are limited only by the group's imagination, and will no doubt include some dubious, if non-existent, shades—all but the most outrageous of which, the host will let pass.

Prizes can be given for the longest list.

COLOR LISTS

Reds

titian	tomato	peach
ruby	cherry	cerise
rose	magenta	maroon
pink	beet	wine
scarlet	burgundy	brick
vermilion	cardinal	rust
crimson	carnation	Chinese red
fuchsia	cinnabar	claret
salmon	lobster	ocher
watermelon	copper	cordovan
strawberry		

Whites

lily white	oyster	oatmeal
chalk	waxy	eggshell
milk white	cream	snow
sand	pearl	albino
off-white	alabaster	silver
blond	bone white	platinum
champagne		

Blues

powder blue	azure	turquoise
aquamarine	navy	royal
sky blue	robin's egg	teal
Prussian	cobalt	cornflower
peacock	delft	gentian
indigo	hyacinth	midnight
electric blue	baby blue	cerulean

SURVIVAL

5-15 players

Props: papers and pencils
Prize

Guests are asked to imagine themselves having survived a plane crash or shipwreck in the wilderness area they would most hate, such as the Yukon, the Amazon jungle, the Gobi desert, a mountaintop, or a remote island. At the last minute they were able to rescue five items of their choice from the plane or ship. The question is, what would those items be?

Papers and pencils are handed out and guests are asked to list, anonymously, the five items they grabbed to help them survive in their particular wilderness. The place is not mentioned.

At the end of five minutes, papers are gathered by the host and redistributed. As guests take turns reading each other's lists, each paper is assigned a number. Players try to guess who wrote each list and what part of the world the writer became stranded in. (Players can write down their guesses on the backs of the sheets handed them.)

A prize can be given to the person with the greatest number of correct guesses.

Plan to be surprised at the denouement by the spouse who says, "I never knew you considered a mountaintop the worst possibility," or the seemingly unimaginative person who comes up with five highly original survival items.

CAPTIONS

5-15 players

Props: 2 or 3 odd or funny pictures (see samples), papers and pencils

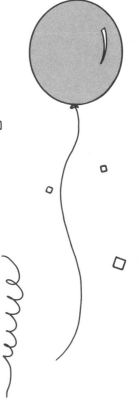

The object of this game is for guests to create humorous captions for the pictures, in the way that graffiti sometimes adds humor to public billboards. This game provides an opportunity for all those budding humorists to come up with their own clever one-liners.

The toughest assignment is finding the right pictures. But they do appear in newspapers from time to time, and there are always the cartoons from syndicated cartoonists. (You can blank out the cartoonist's own caption.) Each guest may be given one of the pictures. After a set time, the captions are exchanged and read aloud. Players can vote on the most fitting caption.

WIDGETS

5-25 players

Props: 5 to 10 unusual objects of generally unknown use and origin which can be passed from hand to hand (see sample), papers and pencils

From time to time all of us have run across odd-shaped implements whose purpose is either unknown or so limited that few people recognize them. We now have a collection of these "widgets" which we've saved specifically for this game.

The widgets are numbered and passed among the crowd. Players examine the items briefly and write down their imagined purpose.

The denouement is the most interesting part of the game. A gadget to turn vegetables into flowers, for instance, can look like anything from a corkscrew to a small drill. Your guests' wild flights of imagination and the revelations of the true identities of these objects are the real objects of the game.

1. medical instrument
2. kidney stone strainer
3. plastic bag hanger
4. orange juice spout
5. vegetable flower maker

6. hemostat
7. plastic hose connector
8. plastic ski pole clip
9. sealing wax rod
10. shoe button hook

ARTIFACTS

5-20 players

Props: 10 common household items, such as lipstick, a bandage, scissors, fork, a piece of string, etc., (see sample), pencils and small slips of paper
Prizes

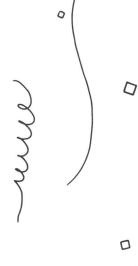

The host appears with a tray of common items and sets them in the center of the room. Guests are then told to imagine that they are uncivilized primatives seeing these objects for the first time. What are they used for?

On separate pieces of paper, players write their names and the name of the object and its new use, such as, lipstick: used for leaving messages on rocks; or scissors: a weapon to stab your enemy.

When everyone has recorded new uses on their papers, the host gathers up all the papers and sorts them into piles by object: all the scissors in one pile, all the lipsticks in another. Each pile goes to a different guest. Guests read the various new uses for each item, then vote on the one best use for each object.

A prize goes to the person who succeeds in winning the most votes.

1. lipstick
2. screw driver
3. piece of string
4. scissors
5. plastic bandage
6. eyeglasses
7. hair brush
8. mirror
9. rolling pin
10. ice pick

EMBARRASSING MOMENTS

15-50 players

Props: none

This game works well with a large crowd.

The host takes any three people aside and asks them to caucus in another room. The three are to discuss embarrassing moments in their lives and choose one which all three will claim to have experienced personally, but in different ways.

Meanwhile, the remaining guests are divided into two teams.

On their return to the group, the three people all give different versions of a single embarrassing moment. For example one man might say, "I walked into the living room naked and our young, teenage babysitter was there and she said, 'Oh, Sir!' " Or, from a woman, "I walked into the kitchen naked and the milkman was there and he said, 'Did you want anything besides milk?' " Or, from another woman, "I walked out onto the service porch naked and the bottled water man was there and he asked, 'Am I here on the right day?' "

After the three versions are told, each team huddles with its members and decides which of the three people is telling the truth. A point goes to the winning team.

The game can be repeated a few times more until one team has gathered 3 (or 5) points.

The winning team will usually opt to go on playing, but as in all games, it's best to stop while enthusiasm is high.

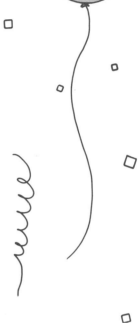

COLOR SEMANTICS

5-15 players

Props: rug samples of various shades or hues (or fabric swatches, colored spools of thread, or any group of similar items which come in a range of shades), papers and pencils
Prize

The object of the game is to find a true semanticist, by majority decision.

The objects are numbered and passed from hand to hand. Guests write down the numbers and give each color a label—the most accurate label possible—such as, cinnamon, burnt orange, tangerine, peach, cerise, wheat, royal purple.

At the end, all descriptions of item #1 are read aloud and compared. Each guest gets a point for every label with which another guest agrees. For instance, if someone calls a color burnt orange and five other guests agree, he or she gets five points for that answer.

The process is repeated with each item, and at the end the winning semanticist is the person who has garnered the greatest number of points. That person, who has found consensus within the group, gets a prize.

PYRAMID PROSE

5-20 players

Props: 2 or 3 sheets of legal-size paper (depending on size of crowd), pencils

The object of this game is to create one or more jointly written stories for the entertainment of the group.

The guests are divided into two or three teams. (No more than 5 to a team so the story will move quickly.)

Papers are handed to the leader in each group, who writes the opening line for a "Great Novel."

The next person on each team reads the opening line, adds a sentence, then folds the paper so at least most of the first sentence is no longer visible.

Each person in turn adds his own line or sentence to the story and folds the paper so that the next writer has only one complete sentence to build on.

The host decides in advance how many "rounds" will be written for each story—two, three or four. Later, the host warns the group when the last round is coming up, so the appropriate "finishing words" can be recorded.

Afterward, one of the guests reads the entire story aloud.

With the right mix of people, the result will be well worth the effort.

FRESH STARTS

10-20 players

Props: a tray with ten familiar, brand-name items, all numbered, (see suggested list), pencils and papers
Prize

The host places the tray of items in the center of the room and announces that various manufacturing companies want to double the sales of their products by giving them new names. Guests are to think up new names, and the most creative guest will be hired immediately to head up a multi-million dollar company.

Guests are then given pencils and papers and allowed 10 or 15 minutes to dream up new names for each product. For instance, Kleenex might be called, "blowies," or Scotch Tape, "French Cling."

At the end, papers are exchanged and guests vote on the best new name for each object. The winner is the person whose names garner the greatest number of votes.

1. Coke
2. Kleenex
3. Bandaid
4. Scotch Tape
5. Pampers
6. Kool-Aid
7. Velcro
8. Liquid Paper
9. Twizzers
10. Thesaurus

TELEGRAM! TELEGRAM!

5-20 players

Props: papers and pencils

After passing out paper and pencils, the host reads a "telegram" which, had it been delivered on time, would have changed the course of history. "To Paul Revere: Dear Paul. The British have changed their minds."

Guests are asked to create their own telegrams which might have changed the course of world events.

After fifteen minutes, telegrams are exchanged and read aloud. The only object of this game is a few minutes of interesting speculation about how a few words at the right time might have affected history.

MALAPROPISMS

5-20 players

Props: pencils and papers

This is another game whose sole object is exploring the guests' creativity.

Each player is asked to write half of a famous saying on a piece of paper, such as, *A stitch in time, He who laughs last* or *The grass is always greener.*

Papers are then passed to the left and players write a new second half for the famous saying. For instance, *A stitch in time . . .* is all right if you're anesthetized, *He who laughs last . . .* didn't get the joke or *The grass is always greener . . .* in someone else's closet.

Depending on the size of the crowd, the papers might be passed left more than once, each time for a new ending to an old saying.

At the end the sayings are read aloud and guests can vote on the one best malapropism.

ANTS UNLIMITED

2-10 players

Props: none

An informal game for small groups of people, this game is a "must" for anyone who loves words. Because no props are needed, it can be played spontaneously in a car or around a dinner table. Thanks to the fact that "ant" appears in more English words than anyone would ever imagine, the game seems almost limitless. Once hooked on it, people find themselves playing it over and over.

The object is simple. One person gives a synonym for— or definition of— a word containing the smaller word "ant" and the rest of the players try to guess the word. "Ant" can appear anywhere in the larger word— beginning, middle or end. The person who guesses first (often loudest) takes his turn defining a new word. And so it goes.

For example, The first player might say, "beggar" and eventually someone would think of "mendicant." Then that person might say "incredible" or "fabulous" and someone will say "fantastic." "Bully" and "despot" would lead to "tyrant," and "church hymn" would be an "anthem."

The following lists of words which contain "ant" at the beginning, middle or end are not complete . . . which must be why word lovers keep returning to this game.

"Ant"–beginning	"Ant"–middle	"Ant"–end
Anthem	Fantasy	Pliant
Anthology	Fantastic	Defiant
Antagonist	Plantation	Mendicant
Antics	Mantle	Flagrant
Antebellum	Tantalize	Compliant
Anterior	Tantrum	Militant
Antipathy	Santa	Supplicant
Antithesis	Tantamount	Blatant
Antlers	Enchantment	Truant
Antipodes	Cantaloupe	Plant
Antenna	Philanthropic	Petulant
Anticlimax	Pedantic	Pant
Antacid	Tarantula	Recalcitrant
Ante	Lantern	Miscreant
Anteroom	Pantry	Recant
Anticipate	Banter	Scant
Antiaircraft	Bantam	Supplant
Anthrax	Tarantella	Want
Antibiotic	Planter	Tyrant
Antimony	Pantaloon	Giant

WORSE FOR WEAR

5-25 players

Props: list of topics, (see samples), papers and pencils
Prizes

Guests are divided into teams of two players. Each team gets a paper and pencil.

The host then asks each pair to jot down 5 topics chosen in advance, leaving space between, such as *clothes . . . love . . . beauty . . . war . . . money . . .* On the call of *Go*, teams are to pick a single topic and write down all the cliches they can think of that relate to it. For instance, *Clothes make the man* or *Beauty is only skin deep.* There will be a strict time limit of 5 minutes.

Each pair can use only one subject as their theme and points will be awarded only to the cliches that nobody else has thought of. So picking the easiest topic isn't necessarily the best way to go.

At the end of 5 minutes, answers are read aloud and prizes awarded to the team that came up with the greatest number of unused cliches.

Topics

1. clothes
2. men
3. women
4. beauty
5. love
6. home
7. money
8. pride
9. children
10. war
11. peace
12. death
13. work
14. happiness

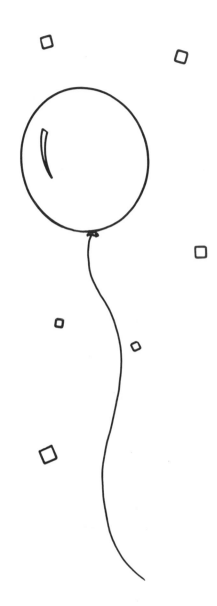

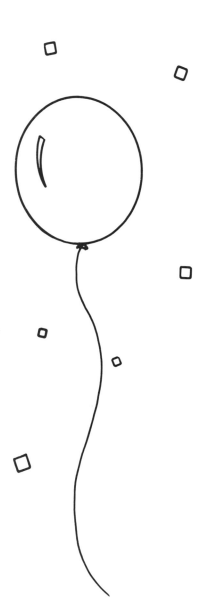

CHAPTER 4

BRAIN GAMES

Brain games should be used sparingly and alternated with *group-participation* games. The purpose is never to single out the brilliant or less-than-brilliant guest, but only to provide some challenging moments and an alternative to other kinds of activities.

It has been our experience that most of these games—especially the more challenging ones—are best played in teams. Not only does a lively sense of camaraderie develop within the group, but nobody is made to feel inadequate. In fact, quite the opposite occurs. Members of a group tend to be inordinately grateful to teammates who contribute answers and help them "win."

Forming up teams is easy. If the host wants five groups, he or she begins a process of "counting off," in which guests number themselves from one to five, then start over at one. All the "ones" become a team, the "twos" likewise, and so on. The advantage of doing it this way is that teams are always a mixed bag, instead of cliques comprised of the people who prefer standing together.

At the end of any brain game, it's important to let winning guests give the correct answers. As always, party games are made better when the guests feel they're running them.

THE ROUNDED BRAIN

5-50 players

Props: quiz sheet with blanks (see sample), pencils
Prizes

The key to *The Rounded Brain* is to choose questions that come from a variety of sources. The quiz offered below is one example, but the possibilities are endless. In general, the greater the range of questions, the more the guests will enjoy it, since almost everyone has some area of expertise. This is one of the few brain games that is best played by individuals instead of teams. As a team game it would probably be too easy.

QUIZ

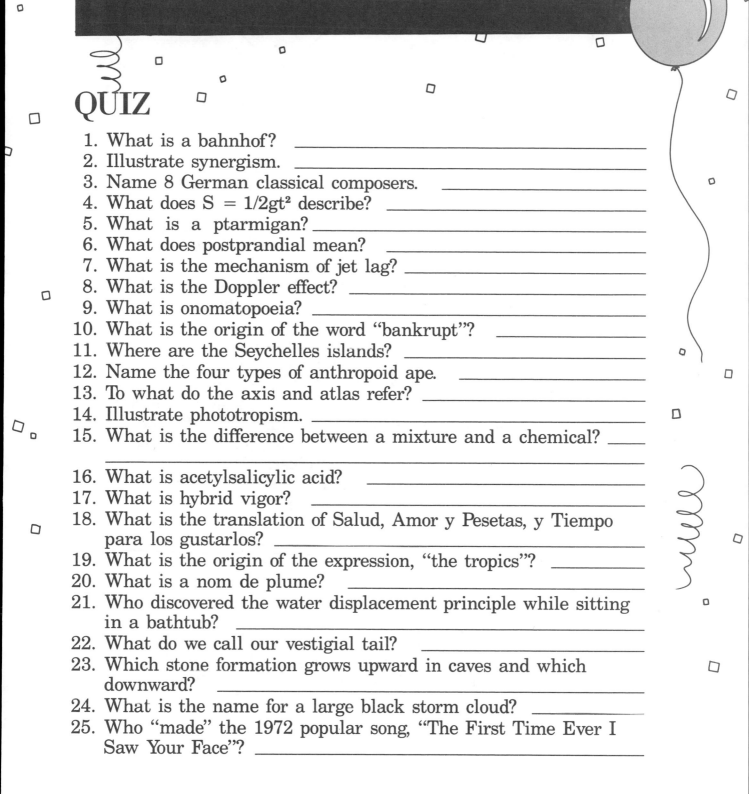

1. What is a bahnhof? _____
2. Illustrate synergism. _____
3. Name 8 German classical composers. _____
4. What does $S = 1/2gt^2$ describe? _____
5. What is a ptarmigan? _____
6. What does postprandial mean? _____
7. What is the mechanism of jet lag? _____
8. What is the Doppler effect? _____
9. What is onomatopoeia? _____
10. What is the origin of the word "bankrupt"? _____
11. Where are the Seychelles islands? _____
12. Name the four types of anthropoid ape. _____
13. To what do the axis and atlas refer? _____
14. Illustrate phototropism. _____
15. What is the difference between a mixture and a chemical? _____
    _____
16. What is acetylsalicylic acid? _____
17. What is hybrid vigor? _____
18. What is the translation of Salud, Amor y Pesetas, y Tiempo para los gustarlos? _____
19. What is the origin of the expression, "the tropics"? _____
20. What is a nom de plume? _____
21. Who discovered the water displacement principle while sitting in a bathtub? _____
22. What do we call our vestigial tail? _____
23. Which stone formation grows upward in caves and which downward? _____
24. What is the name for a large black storm cloud? _____
25. Who "made" the 1972 popular song, "The First Time Ever I Saw Your Face"? _____

MY GRANDMOTHER LIKES

5-30 players

Props: none

There are numerous games of this type around, in which the object is to try to figure out the underlying principle and become a member of the "in" crowd who understands what's going on.

As the game progresses, guests become increasingly eager to reveal the secret to those still in the dark, and some will eventually go to great and sometimes hilarious lengths to make the secret known.

My Grandmother Likes is started by the host saying something like, "My grandmother likes boots but not shoes." If others understand the game, they will add something like, "My grandmother likes walls but not ceilings." As guests gradually catch on, they will chime in with additional likes and dislikes.

It turns out that grandmother likes all words with double letters—it's as simple as that!

However, participants will be thrown off when those in the know choose words that are related in some way. For example, grandmother likes pills but not medicine, feet but not shoes, apples but not oranges, hills but not slopes, wood but not oak or daddy but not dad.

Everyone begins to appreciate the fact that the "brains" of the group are misled into looking for complex relationships when none exist, and most find the game interesting even when they've played it before.

PSYCHO

6-20 players

Props: none

This game is best played by a small group of people who know each other fairly well. The object is to give a few smart players the chance to figure out the game's underlying principle for the amusement of everyone else.

The host explains that the assembled group—all mentally ill—suffers from a common delusion and that three brilliant psychologists are needed to diagnose the illness. He or she asks for three volunteers to assume the roles of psychologists, and these three are sent out of the room.

With the three "psychologists" gone, the host points out that the group's common illness is that they all believe they are the person to their left—and that all questions are to be answered truthfully from that person's viewpoint.

The three "shrinks" are called back and instructed to find the common delusion by asking questions of the other players. However, questions can only be answered with *Yes* or *No.* It is up to the "doctors" to ask the right questions until the common delusion is found.

There is no secondary goal to the game, beyond the enjoyment of watching the three uninformed players struggling to discover what's wrong with the group.

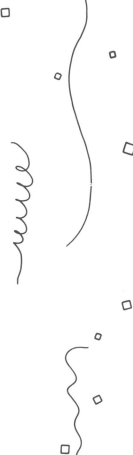

LINGERING LINES

5-50 players

Props: copies of Lingering Lines with blank spaces for names (see sample), pencils
Prize

This quiz, which can be played individually or in groups, consists of quotes which have been made famous by people currently in the news, or quotes so noteworthy they've survived the generations. For instance, "Ask not what your country can do for you; ask what you can do for your country," is a quote that has long succeeded John F. Kennedy.

This game should delight guests who are challenged more by current events than trivia. A prize goes to the guest with the greatest number of correct answers.

WHO SAID THIS?

1. "You won't have me to kick around any more." _____
2. "Come home, America." _____
3. "A choice, not an echo." _____
4. "Let me make this perfectly clear . . ." _____
5. "If you can't stand the heat, get out of the kitchen." _____
6. "I promise you mothers your sons will never fight on foreign soil again." _____
7. "I have a black, a woman, two Jews and a cripple." _____
8. "I hope all you doctors are good Republicans." _____
9. "Ask not what your country can do for you; ask what you can do for your country." _____
10. "I'll stand at the schoolhouse door." _____
11. "I hate war and Eleanor hates war." _____
12. "Come, let us reason together." _____
13. "We will bury you." _____
14. "That's one small step for a man, one giant leap for mankind." _____
15. "I have a dream." _____
16. "Old soldiers never die, they just fade away." _____
17. "A chicken in every pot." _____
18. "Never in the history of the British Empire have so few done so much for so many." _____
19. "God must have loved the common man, he made so many of them." _____
20. "I will not accept if nominated, and will not serve if elected." _____
21. "If the British Empire should endure for a thousand years, historians will still say, 'This was their finest hour.'" _____
22. "Speak softly and carry a big stick." _____
23. "Don't change horses in the middle of the stream." _____
24. "I shall return." _____
25. "Frankly, my dear, I don't give a damn." _____

81

FOX-GRAIN-GOOSE

5-15 players

Props: one copy of the Fox-Grain-Goose problem (see sample)

This game works well in an intimate group. The host presents the "problem" and the guests put their heads together to solve it.

The problem is an interesting one—that of a farmer trying to transport a goose, some grain and a fox across a river without the goose eating the grain or the fox eating the goose—reminiscent of the occasions in which two of us have tried to move an excess of luggage across an airport without leaving any of it unguarded at either end.

A certain amount of logic is required and guests enjoy puzzling out the problem aloud. Finding the solution as a group brings a kind of "think tank" satisfaction.

A man has a fox, a goose and a sack of grain. He must get them all across the river in a boat which will hold only himself plus one of the other three objects. Since, if left unguarded, the fox will eat the goose and the goose will eat the grain, how is he to transport all three without disaster?

The solution requires four trips. First, the man transports the goose across, leaving the fox and grain in relative safety together.

Then he goes back and brings the grain across, and on his return trip takes the goose back with him.

He leaves the goose at the starting point and takes the fox back across the river, leaving it with the grain.

On his last trip he brings the goose over to the other two—having left none of the wrong combinations un-guarded at either end.

SCISSORS

6-40 players

Props: a pair of scissors

This is a logic game. The purpose is to discover the game's underlying principle, which is much simpler than everyone thinks.

Guests are seated in a circle, with their hosts next to each other. One of the pair passes the other the scissors with an elaborate gesture saying, "I'm passing the scissors open," or "I'm passing the scissors closed." Whichever is said, guests will observe that the scissors may, in fact, be the opposite of what has been stated.

The person receiving the scissors says, "I received the scissors *open* and I'm passing them *closed*." Again guests will observe that this may or may not be the case.

But each guest in turn, while receiving and passing the scissors, declares that he received and is passing on the scissors either open or closed. It is the duty of the party givers to inform each guest that he or she is—or isn't—making a correct statement. "That's right," or "That's wrong" or "that's half right."

In the beginning guests are as mystified by being "right" as they are when declared "wrong."

The rightness and wrongness turns out to be simple. Players whose knees are crossed when they are handed the scissors are deemed to receive the scissors "closed." Those whose legs are not crossed, receive the scissors "open." The same goes with passing the scissors on.

The fun begins when 1 or 2 players catch on and begin passing the scissors with correct explanations. As the light dawns with more and more guests, those still in the dark become increasingly frustrated. It is up to the hosts, then, to make the rule increasingly obvious—by crossing and uncrossing their legs elaborately as they receive or pass the scissors. Other guests usually follow suit, and the resulting pantomime can be hilarious.

In the end it is mandatory to give clues so no one will leave unsatisfied.

CELEBRITY NAMES

5-35 players

Props: none

This is another of those circle games that requires such quick thinking and constant attention it can almost be called an action game. But not quite.

The overall purpose is merely to "stay alive" as long as possible by being ready with a correct answer. With everyone seated around a circle, the game begins when one player is asked to call out the name of a celebrity— which can be anyone known by most of the guests. The celebrity can be real or fictional, dead or alive.

As soon as the name is spoken, the rest of the group begins counting aloud, from 1 to 10. The next person in line then has until the count of 10 to respond with another famous name, the only requirement being that the person's first name begin with the same letter as the prior person's last name. For example, Katharine Hepburn could be followed by Howard Cosell, followed by Charlie Brown and then by Babe Ruth. Obviously, people with only one name like Madonna or Cher would be wrong answers. Also, no name can be used twice during the course of one game.

Each time a new person is ready to respond with a name, the group starts over with its counting aloud. Whenever someone misses by coming up with an incorrect name, or no name, he or she is eliminated and the game goes on.

As players drop out, things get pretty tense and the remaining players have to think faster and faster as their turns come around more quickly, which makes the game almost as interesting to the spectators as the participants.

The last person left alive in this shoot-out deserves a good prize.

DOUBLE YOUR TROUBLE

6-30 players

Props: list of categories (list follows), papers and pencils
Prizes

This is a quiz in which two-player teams are given 15 seconds to come up with a maximum of words in a category, such as *names of birds, names of oceans or seas, names of famous villains or traitors, real or fictitious.*

Although the pairs can choose which category they wish to work in, categories are grouped *A, B* and *C,* in descending order of difficulty, with 3 points for each answer in the *A* category, 2 points for answers in *B* and 1 for answers in *C.* But it often happens that one of the pair has expertise in a harder category—a wrinkle which makes the game interesting.

Teams are chosen by numbering off. After the teams are given paper and pencils, the host announces the available categories and the teams quickly decide which category they'll work in.

"Start" is called. For fifteen seconds the teams write down as many words in their category as they can, while the room becomes a virtual beehive of murmuring voices.

"Stop" is called and teams write their names on the papers. Papers are redistributed and answers read aloud, giving the group a chance to invalidate wrong answers, which can provoke lively debate.

Prizes are given for the two highest scores—or else a second round is played with new categories and the highest cumulative scores rewarded.

Topics for A Category

names of famous villains or
traitors, real or fictitious
Cabinet officers
names of famous real or fictitious animals
names of present heads of
state
types of musical compositions
countries or republics in
Africa
various adjectives designating
shades of red
names of publishing houses
flowers beginning with *P*
names of planets
names of Russian composers
famous artists
types of poisonous snakes
Indian tribes

Topics for B Category

names of oceans or seas
foods which grow
underground
first names, U.S. presidents
spirits or liquors
names of famous battles
TV brand names

names of evergreen trees
football bowl games
names of card games
Shakespearean characters
names of berries
chemical elements
famous inventors
airlines

Topics for C Category

names of birds
Walt Disney characters
animals with claws
names of diseases
sports where a ball is used
names of trees
names of religions
fur-bearing animals
expressions of greeting
precious stones
brands of watches
magazines with one-
word titles
names of fruits
breeds of dogs

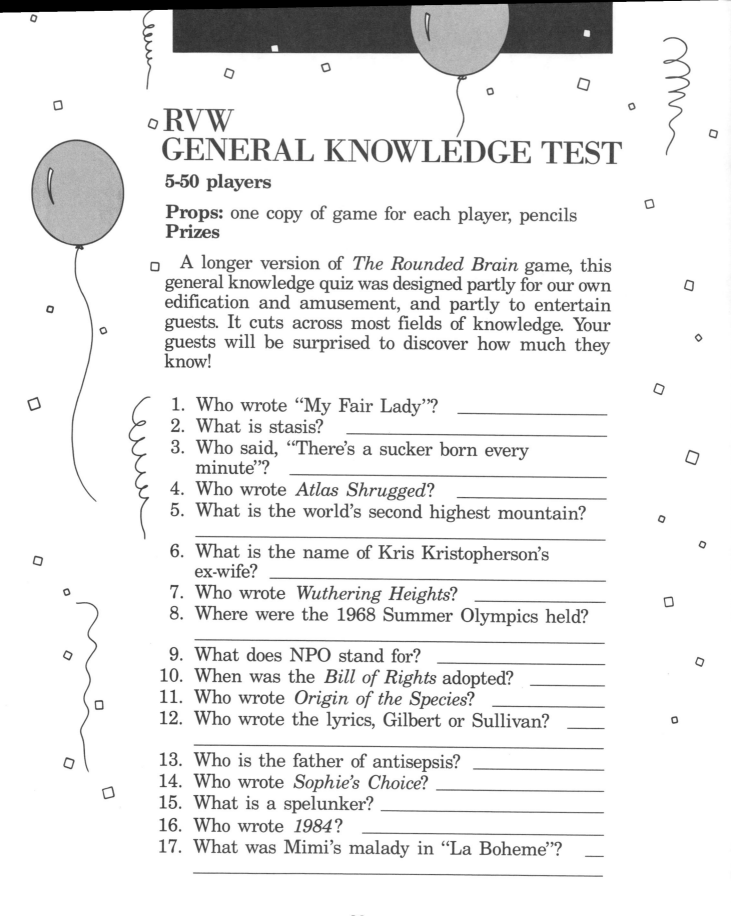

RVW
GENERAL KNOWLEDGE TEST

5-50 players

Props: one copy of game for each player, pencils
Prizes

A longer version of *The Rounded Brain* game, this general knowledge quiz was designed partly for our own edification and amusement, and partly to entertain guests. It cuts across most fields of knowledge. Your guests will be surprised to discover how much they know!

1. Who wrote "My Fair Lady"? _____
2. What is stasis? _____
3. Who said, "There's a sucker born every minute"? _____
4. Who wrote *Atlas Shrugged*? _____
5. What is the world's second highest mountain? _____
6. What is the name of Kris Kristopherson's ex-wife? _____
7. Who wrote *Wuthering Heights*? _____
8. Where were the 1968 Summer Olympics held? _____
9. What does NPO stand for? _____
10. When was the *Bill of Rights* adopted? _____
11. Who wrote *Origin of the Species*? _____
12. Who wrote the lyrics, Gilbert or Sullivan? _____
13. Who is the father of antisepsis? _____
14. Who wrote *Sophie's Choice*? _____
15. What is a spelunker? _____
16. Who wrote *1984*? _____
17. What was Mimi's malady in "La Boheme"? __
_____

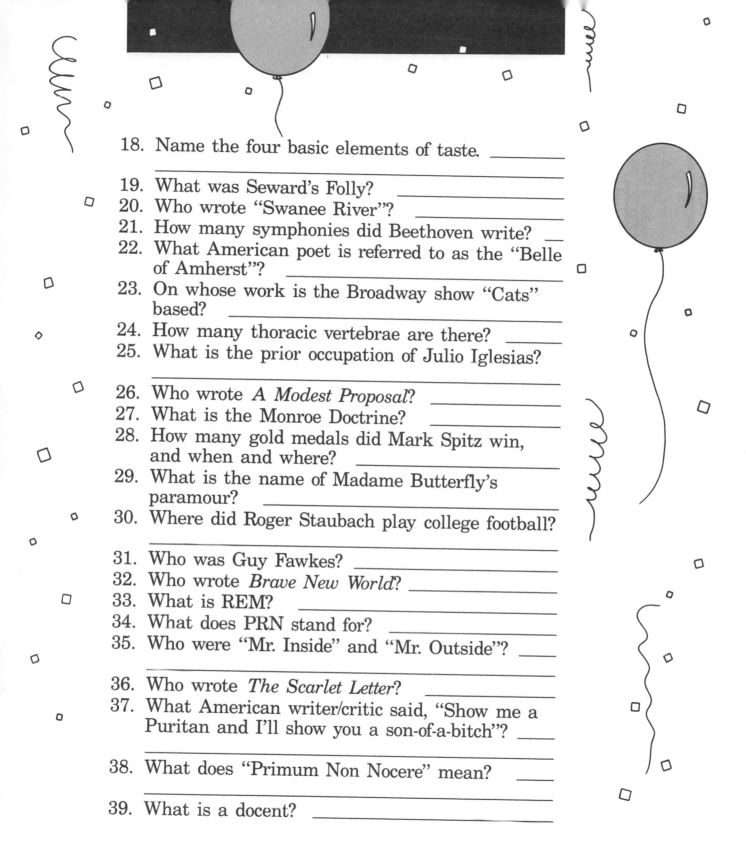

18. Name the four basic elements of taste. _____
    _____
19. What was Seward's Folly? _____
20. Who wrote "Swanee River"? _____
21. How many symphonies did Beethoven write? __
22. What American poet is referred to as the "Belle of Amherst"? _____
23. On whose work is the Broadway show "Cats" based? _____
24. How many thoracic vertebrae are there? _____
25. What is the prior occupation of Julio Iglesias?
    _____
26. Who wrote *A Modest Proposal*? _____
27. What is the Monroe Doctrine? _____
28. How many gold medals did Mark Spitz win, and when and where? _____
29. What is the name of Madame Butterfly's paramour? _____
30. Where did Roger Staubach play college football?
    _____
31. Who was Guy Fawkes? _____
32. Who wrote *Brave New World*? _____
33. What is REM? _____
34. What does PRN stand for? _____
35. Who were "Mr. Inside" and "Mr. Outside"? ____
    _____
36. Who wrote *The Scarlet Letter*? _____
37. What American writer/critic said, "Show me a Puritan and I'll show you a son-of-a-bitch"? ____
    _____
38. What does "Primum Non Nocere" mean? ____
    _____
39. What is a docent? _____

RARE BIRDS

5-30 players

Props: prepared sheets with categories and blank squares, pencils
Prize

You will see that each of the sample sheets has a key word down the left side. The object is to fill in the squares with an appropriate word that begins with the letter on the left—but more than that, to come up with an original word that nobody else has thought of.

Players are given 5 minutes to fill in all the blanks they can. At the end the host asks for guests' answers by category, and those guests having an exclusive answer give themselves 10 points per answer. Those sharing an answer with one other person get 5 points. One point is given for every answer shared by more than one other person.

Being original is not easy. Often two or three people come up with the same obscure word, leaving more obvious ones untouched.

This game is best played individually instead of in teams. The denouement is usually the best part of the game; guests get a lot of satisfaction out of scooping each other with odd or farfetched answers.

On page 91 are easy *Rare Birds* and on page 92 they are more difficult.

Directions: *Fill in the squares with one answer beginning with the letter on the left column. Scoring is as follows: Ten points for answers no one else has. Five points for answers shared by one other person. One point for answers shared by more than one other person.*

	Feminine Names	Trees	Animals	Movie Stars (Last Names)
H				
O				
L				
I				
D				
A				
Y				

	Flowers	Colors	Authors (Last Names)	Fruits or Vegetables
H				
O				
S				
P				
I				
T				
A				
L				

NOTORIOUS NUMBERS

5-50 players

Props: *Notorious Numbers* quiz sheet—one for each team, pencils
Significant Prizes

This is the granddaddy of challenging puzzles, which is why we've saved it for last. It is so hard that my husband and I worked on it, intermittently, for weeks and still left two or three items unsolved. It wasn't until we presented the game at a party that the last answers came to light.

As a team game this quiz is both fun and thought provoking. As a quiz for individuals it could bring your party to a horrible, shuddering stop.

Even as a team endeavor, it's best to have at least seven members on a team, and it helps if the teams cover a range of ages. With this quiz you need all the input you can get!

Directions: *Find the words behind the mystery initials. Use the numbers to find a common—or not so common—expression. For example, 2P in a Q = 2 pints in a quart.*

1 H on a U _____

2 H are B than O _____

3 S and Y O _____

4 W and the S S _____

5 P on a B T _____

6 P on the S of D _____

7 D and S W _____

8 B and A W _____

9 S by B _____

10 Y for a F D _____

11 P on a S T _____

12 M in a Y _____

13 C in a B H _____

14 S of the C _____

15 P B (not counting the C B) _____

16 O in a P _____

17 Y L _____

18 Y O to V _____

19th H of a G C _____

20 C in a P _____

21 G S _____

26 M in a M _____

30 D hath S, A, J and N _____

32 T in the M _____

40 T and A B _____

50 S in the U _____

60 S in a M _____

100 C in a D _____

101 D _____

212 D at which W B _____

360 D in a C _____

5280 F in a M _____

25,000 M around the E _____

SIGN LANGUAGE

5-50 players

Props: one copy of the game for every fifth person, pencils
5 Prizes

Unlike *Cave Language,* which relies on a fixed code, *Sign Language* is a pictorial representation of words or phrases in which each item is unique. However, all the expressions are familiar to everyone. Since this game is quite difficult, it is best played in groups of 5 so guests will have a feeling of success. The object is to be the first team to figure out all 20 clues.

The sample given includes both words and phrases . . . and the host will observe that some are logical and "clean" and others have a pun-like quality, which will probably elicit groans.

Prizes go to the first team completing its sheet.

Identify The Following:

1. <u>EGGS</u>
   EASY

2. S_EC_T_IO_N
   s_EC_T_IO_N

3. ANGLE ANGLE ANGLE

4. PERSON   ALITY

5. <u>RISING</u>
        IT

6. VISION

7. T I M E, ~~SEE~~

8. <u>STRICTLY</u>
      BOARD

9.   A
    E   P
   S   P
    U   L
         A

10. CLASS

11. BAKED

12. TAKE TAKE

13. GROUND

14. [ICE]

15. S
    T
    A
    I
    R
    S

16. <u>GLASS</u>
    PHEASANT

17. IT'S / THE POINT

18. T
    A
    L
    E

19. TIMER TIMER

20. HEART

21. <u>BACK</u>
     TOP

22. <u>LONG</u>
     DUE

23. L A D E P

24. <u>BRIDGE</u>
    WATER

25. O
     V
      E
       R

97

FACT OR FANCY

5-50 players

Props: copies of *Fact or Fancy* sheet, one for each guest (see sample), pencils

This game is not quite as "automatic" as it appears. Even logical thinkers can slip on this one.

Each guest is handed a pencil and a copy of the game, and the group is given a time limit of 5 minutes.

When time is called, the host asks for guests' opinions of which statements on the sheet are fact and which inference. The denouement can result in a pretty lively discussion as to where fact leaves off and inference begins.

"Wallace, Chief Executive Officer at United Lumber, was down on the books for an 11 o'clock meeting in Mr. Johnson's office to discuss proposals for a new stand of timber. On the way to that office, Wallace developed a severe allergic reaction and was having trouble breathing. By the time Johnson was notified of the incident, Wallace was on the way to the hospital for an injection. Johnson called the hospital to inquire, but couldn't find anyone who could tell him about Wallace. The emergency room nurse had never heard the name. Johnson wondered if he'd called the wrong hospital."

On the basis of the information given above, please mark each of the following statements as *fact* or *inference*.

Fact: a statement that is true, based on the facts given above.

Inference: a statement that is merely *implied* from the above true information.

_____ 1. Mr. Wallace is a Chief Executive Officer.

_____ 2. Wallace was supposed to meet with Johnson.

_____ 3. Wallace was on the books for an 11 o'clock meeting.

_____ 4. The incident occurred at United Lumber.

_____ 5. Wallace was taken to the hopital for an injection.

_____ 6. No one at the hospital which Johnson called knew anything about Wallace.

_____ 7. Johnson had called the wrong hospital.

PLANET EARTH QUIZ

5-20 players

Props: one or more copies of *Planet Earth Quiz*

We generally ask our guests these questions informally and in a relaxed, non-competitive manner. It is a quiz designed to engender thoughtful discussion and bring up geographical facts which aren't generally known. Most of our guests are happy if they know a third of the answers.

Before You Head For Space, How Much Do You Know About Planet Earth?

A score of 15 is pretty good; 17 is excellent; 18 or above astronomical.

1. What body of water lies between Saudi Arabia and Africa?
2. Name 4 major cities in South Africa.
3. Where is the Isle of Man?
4. Name the principal port and trading center of Malaysia.
5. Where is Tasmania?
6. Which is farther north, Greece or Southern California?
7. What other major countries have flags that are red, white and blue?
8. What is the current name of the island we knew as Ceylon?
9. What is the capital of Bulgaria?
10. What do the Chinese call the Chinese capital city?
11. What 2 nations make up the island known as Hispaniola?
12. What is the capital of Afghanistan?
13. Where and what is Lapland?
14. Name the capital of Malaysia.
15. Where and what are the Tropic of Cancer and the Tropic of Capricorn?
16. Dacca (Dhaka) is the capital of what country?
17. What is the new name of Cambodia?
18. What is the largest lake in the world?
19. What is the longest river in the world?
20. Where is the country called Belize?
21. Name the highest mountain in Africa.

RVW PERSONALITY PROFILE

6-20 players

Props: copies of the *RVW Personality Profile* for each player, pencils

This has been a long-standing favorite, brought out from time to time to play with new friends. Guests are asked to give honest, thoughtful answers, and not to show them to anyone else. At the end, papers are exchanged among the players and read aloud, and the group tries to guess which paper belongs to whom.

This is one of our most revelatory games. Not only is it interesting to note how often spouses fail to identify each other, but the questions themselves tend to encourage discussion about enlightening though rarely mentioned subjects. Players sometimes remark that a game like this can solidify their viewpoints.

Directions: *Print your best answers after the questions. Answer every question. Do not indicate your name or reveal your answers.*

1. Name your favorite musical composer since 1400 AD.
2. If you were to start your education all over again, what business or profession would you favor?
3. What do you consider the most desirable character or personality trait in a spouse (e.g., loyalty, ambition, veracity, etc.)?
4. What trait do you consider the most intolerable in a spouse?
5. What would you regard as an ideal number of children for a couple living in suburban America?
6. Do you have too much time to yourself, or not enough?
7. Do you feel that Americans overemphasize sports at the expense of academics?
8. What are the three most honorable professions?
9. What is your favorite color?
10. Do you feel that things generally "work out for the best"?
11. Name your favorite actor or actress.
12. Do you prefer fiction or nonfiction books?
13. Who was the best U.S. president since 1900?
14. Do you believe that monogamy is here to stay?
15. Do you believe that late marriages have a better chance of success than early marriages?
16. Which decade of life should be the most enjoyable?
17. Would you rather be male or female?

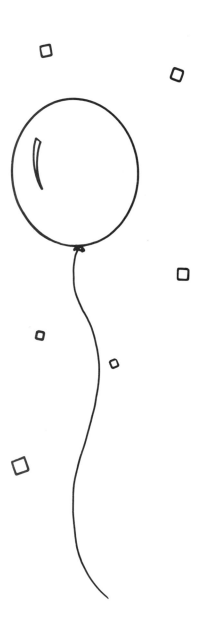

CHAPTER 5

ACTION GAMES

Action games, in addition to being fun, get people up and moving to liven up a quiet party. It's a good idea to include at least one action game in every party, preferably sandwiched between sedentary events. People who sit too long tend to become sleepy.

All of these livelier games work quite well in ordinary living rooms, though a few have been played in ballrooms with over a hundred guests. Oddly, some of the most sophisticated, elegantly dressed people have joined the fray with an abandon that's startling.

BEDLAM

10-40 players

Props: enough slips of paper (each with a single, unique action described, such as *play the violin*) for half the group, duplicates for a second group of players, stopwatch or watch with second hand

This game falls halfway between the *Imagination* and *Action* Categories, but since it's played standing up, we're including it here. The object of the game is to avoid being the last two people playing—which carries some lighthearted penalty, such as having the two losing guests wear a "loser" button, a checkered coat or over-size galoshes—anything that connotes stigma.

Guests are divided into two groups, one group being the "Actors" and the other group the "Guessers." Each person in the acting group is handed a slip of paper describing some bit of action, such as *Ride a Horse, Conduct an Orchestra, Hammer a Nail.* Identical papers are given to the guessers. The two groups form opposing lines, facing each other across the room. The host announces the game will be over in 15 seconds.

On a signal from the host, the actors begin performing their small bits of acting, and it is up to each guesser to decide which person is acting out the instruction on his slip of paper, and run across the room and remove that person from the lineup.

The next 15 seconds are bedlam, as some of the guests are madly repeating their acted-out behaviors, some are searching frantically, and others are dashing across the room to pull someone out of the lineup. At 15 seconds the host shouts, Stop, and everyone still in the lineup freezes.

Actors still playing swap papers and the remaining guessers do the same. The game goes on, except the remaining players have only 10 seconds to perform.

If anyone is still left after 10 seconds, a last round is played with a 5-second time allotment, until only two players are left. These become the grand losers.

pick a cinder out of
  your eye
ride a horse
throw a ball
thread a needle
do a waltz
bat a ball
tie your necktie
ski down a slope
conduct an orchestra
jump rope
fire a rifle
hammer a nail
play a trumpet
waterski
go rollerskating
put on pants
wash your face
eat a lemon
cry like a baby
blow your nose
sew a button
say your prayers
stand in a windstorm

do calisthenics
act bored and sleepy
comb your hair
swing a lasso
pretend you're being
  tickled
fold a sheet
scratch an itch
swim the breaststroke
play hopscotch
type a letter
play a violin
play a harp
dive into a pool
brush your teeth
tug your girdle
tie your shoes
act drunk
get the hiccups
beat an egg
pop a balloon
laugh at a joke
answer the telephone

ROLE PLAYING

10-20 players

Props: enough slips of paper (each containing the name of a distinctive famous person) for half the crowd, duplicate slips for the other half

Simliar to *Bedlam,* but more difficult, this game entails guest/actors pretending they are famous people and attempting to depict them by acting out some well known characteristic or group of characteristics. It is a great deal more subtle and difficult than acting out a simple, uncomplicated instruction. This game usually involves multiple behaviors and will consequently be more difficult to "read."

As in *Bedlam,* actors and guessers alike are handed random slips of paper, the guessers' slips containing the same names as the actors' slips.

Before the game begins, it is best to offer a sample name, such as John Wayne, and discuss how he can be portrayed. The actor might portray him riding a horse, doffing a cowboy hat, shooting a gun.

The actors and guessers line up facing each other, and when told to "Go," the actors begin to portray their celebrity in some way. Actors will be given 2 minutes to accomplish their tasks.

As each guesser locates his actor, they leave the lineup.

Since this game is so difficult, the host might offer prizes to the first three couple successfully pinpointing their famous person.

RHYTHMS

10-30 players

Props: none

Seats are numbered, 1-30, depending on the number of players participating. The number one seat is the *Whip.* The purpose of the game is to work one's way up to the number one seat.

Whip starts the game by initiating a rhythm—slap the knees, clap the hands, snap the fingers, then clap the hands again. As soon as all players have joined the rhythm, the *whip* calls out his own number, "One!" on the slap of the knees, and then some other number, say, "Four!" with the snap of the fingers. Without breaking the rhythm, the person in Seat 4 calls out his own number on the knee slap, then someone else's number at the finger snap. Guests toss the number to each other until someone misses. Then that person goes to the last seat and everyone moves up a seat.

The game requires an array of talents: good concentration, a keen sense of rhythm and a cool head. When one's number is called, there is often a flustered, split second of confusion—first the realization that it's necessary to respond, then the decision as to *how.*

The fun comes when players gang up on the *whip* and keep throwing the number one back at him, trying to rattle him.

Variations can be added when guests become adept. Numbers can be skipped, and anyone calling a missing number is sent to the end of the line. Often guests who have just switched chairs forget their new number and miss immediately.

This is a good game for any age group.

POLLY PARAGON

15-45 players

Props: one copy of the Polly Paragon story (copy follows)

Prizes (enough for one-fifth of the group)

The host introduces this game by explaining that he or she is a casting director looking for actors to put in a spy thriller and since there is so much talent at this party the guests will be asked to try out for roles. Tryouts will be done on a group basis and everyone will vote on which group does the best job.

The host then divides the party loosely into five units, comprised of people sitting near one another, explaining, "This group is *Polly Paragon,* you people are the *Spy,* you the *Cops,*" and so on.

The host further explains the acting talent required of each group. "When I say the words *Polly Paragon,* you stand up, puff out your chest, hold out your hands like a queen, spin around and sit down again." Then the host explains the requirements of the *Spy,* who must stand, put his hand over his eyes and crouch low. Similarly, the host explains the acting required of the *Cops,* the *Helicopter,* and the *Bicycle,* physically demonstrating each role.

The host then reads the story, pausing at the key words to give the designated actors time to leap to their feet to provide the visual effects.

If all this sounds a bit corny, it is. But it is also fun, especially if guests enter into the spirit and do their acting with verve. Most people are amused by the sight of robust males preening like *Polly Paragon,* or ladylike females crouched in the sinister pose of the *Spy.*

At the end the host decides good-naturedly, or asks for a vote, on which group did the best job. Prizes are awarded to the winners.

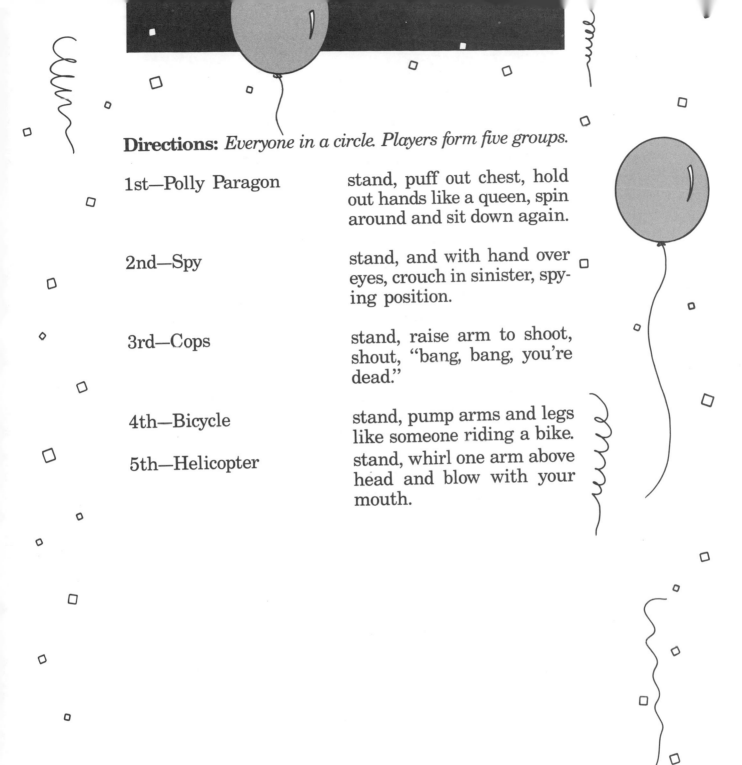

Directions: *Everyone in a circle. Players form five groups.*

1st—Polly Paragon — stand, puff out chest, hold out hands like a queen, spin around and sit down again.

2nd—Spy — stand, and with hand over eyes, crouch in sinister, spying position.

3rd—Cops — stand, raise arm to shoot, shout, "bang, bang, you're dead."

4th—Bicycle — stand, pump arms and legs like someone riding a bike.

5th—Helicopter — stand, whirl one arm above head and blow with your mouth.

POLLY PARAGON STORY

As we read the story, whenever your part is mentioned, you rise, act your part, then sit down as quickly as possible.

In today's world, nobody is safe from the long, grasping fingers of intrigue. When *Polly Paragon* received a solid gold locket, she didn't know her lover was a *Spy*, nor did she know there was a stolen government code inside the locket. Even as she hung the locket around her perfect, swanlike throat, the *Cops* were gathering outside her door.

Hearing a noise, *Polly Paragon* flung open the door. Circling overhead was a police *Helicopter*, and out on her lawn were a dozen *Cops*. "Polly," they cried, "throw us your locket!"

"Never!" she screamed, with her hand on her perfect, swanlike throat.

"Then give us the *Spy*!" they shouted, and she shouted back, "I don't have the *Spy*!"

She ran back inside and escaped out the back door on a *Bicycle*. Furiously she pedaled the *Bicycle* through the town until a man jumped on the back, and she realized she was carrying the *Spy*. "Pedal fast, *Polly Paragon*," he shouted, "the *Cops* are following by *Helicopter*."

She whirled on him. "I don't care, you wicked *Spy*, you're too heavy for this bike! Get off *now*!"

"Never!" shouted the *Spy*, "You're taking me to the border!"

"But," she wailed, "there are even more *Cops* at the border!"

"You fool, *Polly Paragon*," shouted the *Spy*, "They don't want you, and they don't want the locket. They've got enough *Helicopters*. They want the *Bicycle*!"

THE MINISTER'S CAT

10-30 players

Props: none

Guests are seated in a circle and told they will be describing the minister's cat in a variety of ways, working through the letters of the alphabet. For instance, player number one might say, "The minister's cat is an *awful* cat," and player two, "The minister's cat is an *alley* cat." Players in turn will continue to describe the cat with adjectives beginning with *A*, going around the circle until someone misses, after which that person is eliminated and the game goes on beginning with the *B*'s. For example, "The minister's cat is a *brown* cat." When someone trips up over the *B*'s, the game proceeds with *C*.

The catch in this game is that it must be played in rhythm. Players slap their thighs as they say, "The *minister's cat is a bad cat*," and without missing a beat, the next person must describe the cat with another adjective starting with *B*. In the course of searching for adjectives in a hurry, some pretty wild, if not utterly distracting words will come to mind. But nobody still in the game will have time to laugh; that's reserved for the spectators.

Each time someone misses, that person drops out of the game and the game goes on with the next letter of the alphabet until only two people are left. The last two must be pretty cool heads if they hope to continue long.

The good host will reward the last two players with something nice.

ADVERBS

8-30 players

Props: none

The purpose of the game is for one person, the "it," to try to figure out an adverb chosen by the group while he's out of the room. The method is deceptively easy. While "it" is gone, the group chooses an adverb, any adverb, such as *lazily*. Then the Guesser comes back and asks the other players to perform small tasks in the manner of the word, such as, "Stand up in the manner of the word." The player obliges by standing up as lazily as possible.

The "it" may guess or, if he or she isn't sure yet, may ask another player to perform a simple task, such as, "Bring me a glass in the manner of the word."

The game goes on until "it" guesses the word, in which case he gets to choose someone else to be "it." But several rules must be followed: "It" never asks the same person to perform twice, and is allowed only 3 guesses, though "it" may ask for any number of performances "in the manner of the word."

If "it" doesn't guess the adverb in 3 guesses, "it" must go out again on another word.

All kinds of adverbs may be used in this game: *lazily, sleepily, humorously, angrily, pleasantly, gracefully, awkwardly*. Likewise, any number of small actions are possible: sit down in the manner of the word, run in the manner of the word, tie your shoe in the manner of the word, point in the manner of the word.

Two or three rounds of this game will probably be just enough.

BALLOON STOMP

10-40 players

Props: one or two balloons for every guest, an 18-inch piece of string for each guest
Prize or prizes

This is a rather robust game and requires a room which can't be hurt by a lot of stamping feet.

Each guest blows up a balloon, secures it with one end of a string, then ties the free end of the string to his ankle.

The object of the game is to stamp on other people's balloons without having your own attacked—which requires some tricky footwork.

At the call of "Go!", guests begin hopping around after each other, dancing to keep their own balloons off the ground, lunging to attack other people's balloons.

Once a player's balloon is popped he or she must leave the arena. Not surprisingly, players begin popping out in large numbers. This game is as good for spectators as participants!

The final players will invariably surprise you. Along with the known extroverts there will be one or more gentle types whose sudden show of aggressiveness seems to come out of nowhere.

But not to worry. We've never seen any real problems in 25 years of playing this game!

EGG FOOTBALL

6-24 players

Props: four or five fresh eggs "blown out" through tiny holes in the ends, a ping pong table or dining room table which can be marked with chalk at both ends **Team prizes**

Memories of this game date back to a high school party in an echoing gymnasium—and the laughter still rings to this day. The merriment we enjoyed then has been repeated at parties over and over in the intervening years.

The trickiest part of this game is preparing the empty eggs. Before the party starts, several eggs must be prepared by pricking both ends with a needle or pin—several pricks in the same spot—producing a hole about the size of an "O" on a page of ordinary size print. This done, blow into one of the holes vigorously until the contents of the egg dribble out the opposing end. It's not easy to do. The egg is never inclined to part with its contents, and the shell *is* inclined to break if it's treated roughly. Sometimes nothing happens until one of the holes is enlarged.

The object of the game is simple: Teams of squatting or kneeling players at opposite ends of a table attempt to blow the empty egg shell across the chalked goal line of the opposing team. Each team can be composed of as few as three people or as many as six. More players than that tend to get in each other's way.

To start the game, the egg is placed in the center of the table, and from then on can be moved only by lung power. Players are, however, allowed to catch the egg if it threatens to roll off the table—at which point the host places it back in the center. The first team making one or more "goals" is the winner.

The principal rule to keep in mind is that players can't extend their faces past the edge of the table—meaning a lot of group blowing is required to make a goal. The smart player quickly discovers that the secret is to let the egg roll close to his or her face before giving it a strong blast—which will often send the orb rolling away against all efforts to stop it.

As simple as this all sounds, the hilarity evolves from the visual impact of a group of people with red faces and puffed-out cheeks blowing furiously at each other, while the egg between them jumps and spins around erratically, often rolling away as though it had come alive. It's one of those gags you have to see to appreciate.

As an added wrinkle, spectators can take bets on the winning team.

SILVERWARE SYMPHONY

10-40 players

Props: assorted silverware, glasses and cups, copies of *Silverware Symphony* (see sample)

Silverware Symphony is a game to be played at dinner. To the tune of *Country Gardens,* or any other that the host chooses, guests sing and accompany themselves as directed by the "music." The "music" is comprised of knife on fork for 8 counts, then knife on glass for 8.

The host stands at the head of the table with cups, glasses and silverware at hand and leads the singing and the accompanying sound effects. Guests sing along and accompany themselves according to the direction sheet.

There is no point to this game. Just a lot of sound effects which are interesting and often funny, particularly when players must scramble to grab their tools without losing the beat.

1.	Knife on fork	8 counts	11.	Knife on fork	8 counts
2.	Knife on glass	8 counts	12.	Clap	8 counts
3.	Knife on fork	8 counts	13.	Knife on fork	8 counts
4.	Whistle the tune	8 counts	14.	Knife on glass	8 counts
5.	Clap	8 counts	15.	Knife on fork	8 counts
6.	Knife on fork	8 counts	16.	Clap	8 counts
7.	Knife on glass	8 counts	17.	Knife on fork	8 counts
8.	Whistle the tune	8 counts	18.	Knife on glass	8 counts
9.	Knife on fork	8 counts	19.	Knife on fork	8 counts
10.	Knife on glass	8 counts	20.	Whistle the tune	8 counts

10-30 players

Props: none

With guests seated in a circle around the room, the host explains that it's difficult not to be influenced by what those around you are doing—as this game will illustrate.

The host is "it," for a demonstration of the next move and how the players are to respond. "If I come toward you playing a violin, you must pat your head. If I approach patting my head, you must be a mime and pretend you're playing some musical instrument, such as a horn, trombone or violin. If you make a mistake, you become 'it.'"

The host then darts toward one guest after another, gesturing either as a musician or head patter. It becomes almost impossible for the guest not to imitate what the host is doing—especially when rushed at quickly.

As with most games, it is important to play this one only a short time and to stop while guests are still amused.

JENKENS UP, JENKENS DOWN

6-24 players

Props: none

This game is a real old timer. It came to us from an 80-year-old man who played it himself as a child. Introduced to us only recently, we found it both simple and entertaining—a challenging little game of deception to be played at the dinner table during one of those blank intervals that occur before or after dinner.

Team members are decided automatically. All the people on one side of the table are a team and those facing them are another. Somebody produces a coin (we used a quarter) and holds it up for the opposing team to see. Then everybody on that side of the table puts their hands under the table and the coin is passed randomly in one direction or another out of sight of everyone. Nobody, except the person holding the coin, knows where it is.

After letting the coin pass back and forth for a brief time somebody (an arbitrary "Captain") from the opposing team calls out, "Jenkins Up!" and the coin-passers all put their elbows on the table fists closed. The Captain then calls, "Jenkins Down!" and the coin-team all slap their hands onto the table, hoping whoever has the coin won't slap it down too noisily.

Each member of the "Guessing team" then gets one guess as to who holds the coin. Each time a player is asked to open his hands and he comes up coinless, his team earns 5 points. The "guessing players" continue in turn until somebody finds the person with the coin, at which time the coin goes across the table for another round.

Somebody keeps score and the game goes on until something better comes along.

COTTON BALLS

6-15 players

Props: large bowl, two dozen cotton balls, spatula, blindfold
Prizes

Some games are better played with small numbers and this is one of them. Boredom sets in rapidly when participants are forced to wait though a long line of players to take their turns.

The object of this game is for a blindfolded player wielding a spatula to scoop as many cotton balls into a bowl as possible—the problem being that cotton balls are so light the player can't *feel* what is happening.

Some may think this a children's game, which it is. However, adults quickly add new dimensions and therein lies the fun. Instead of fumbling blindly, mature players develop various schemes to solve the problem, and watching them learn as the game progresses is where the entertainment lies.

A player is blindfolded, handed a spatula, and then, while he waits, the host scatters the cotton balls over the floor nearby. The player's hand is directed to the bowl and with a 30-second time limit the player begins trying to maneuver the fluffy stuff into the container. It often happens that the first few players scoop madly and capture nothing. But the host cheers on their attempts, encouraging everyone else to do likewise—which adds an element of surprise when the player removes the blindfold and finds the bowl empty.

Players get smarter. Some begin scraping cotton balls into a pile (they think) and gathering the collected balls in one or two neat moves (they hope). This may give other guests additional ideas for solving the problem.

The time limit is very important. To keep interest high, no guest should be given longer than a minute, and preferably only 30 seconds.

Prizes are awarded to the winners . . . and maybe one to the biggest loser.

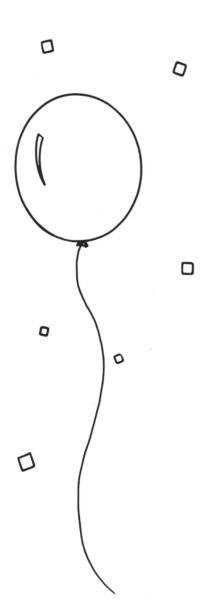

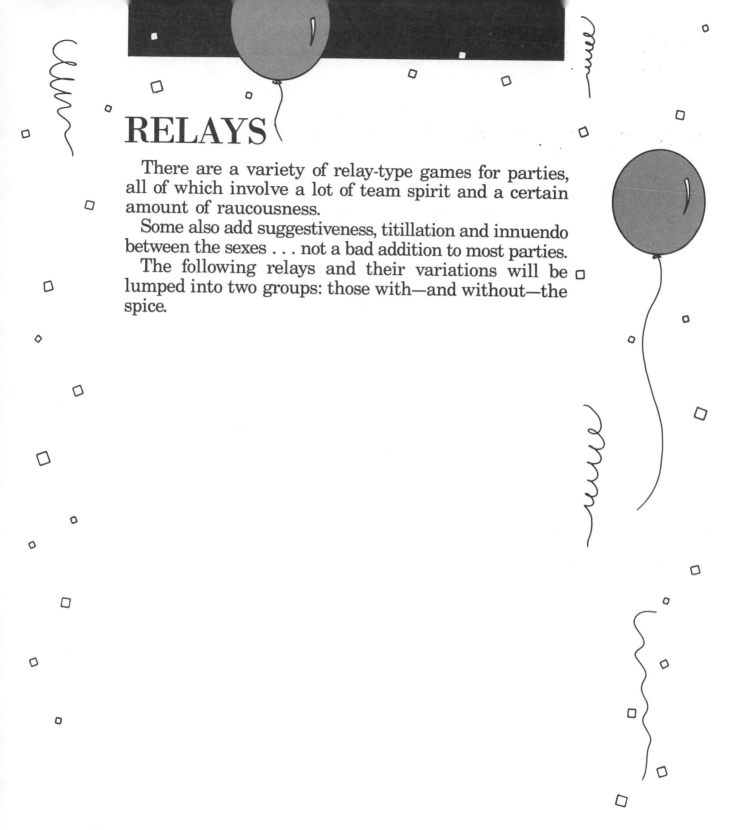

RELAYS

There are a variety of relay-type games for parties, all of which involve a lot of team spirit and a certain amount of raucousness.

Some also add suggestiveness, titillation and innuendo between the sexes . . . not a bad addition to most parties.

The following relays and their variations will be lumped into two groups: those with—and without—the spice.

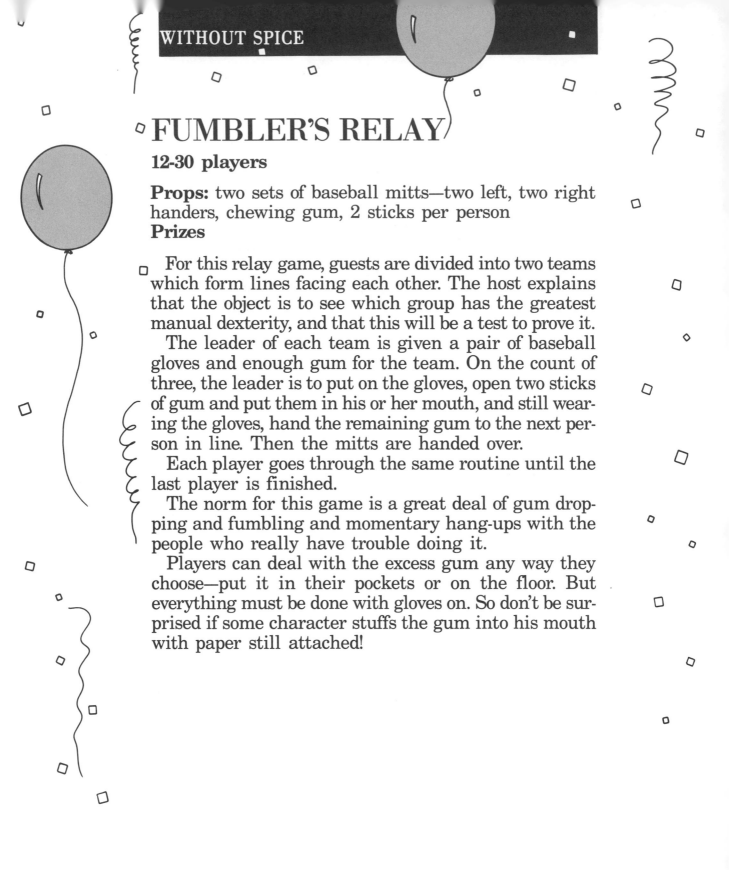

FUMBLER'S RELAY

12-30 players

Props: two sets of baseball mitts—two left, two right handers, chewing gum, 2 sticks per person
Prizes

For this relay game, guests are divided into two teams which form lines facing each other. The host explains that the object is to see which group has the greatest manual dexterity, and that this will be a test to prove it.

The leader of each team is given a pair of baseball gloves and enough gum for the team. On the count of three, the leader is to put on the gloves, open two sticks of gum and put them in his or her mouth, and still wearing the gloves, hand the remaining gum to the next person in line. Then the mitts are handed over.

Each player goes through the same routine until the last player is finished.

The norm for this game is a great deal of gum dropping and fumbling and momentary hang-ups with the people who really have trouble doing it.

Players can deal with the excess gum any way they choose—put it in their pockets or on the floor. But everything must be done with gloves on. So don't be surprised if some character stuffs the gum into his mouth with paper still attached!

FEATHER RELAY

12-30 people

Props: two large spoons, several large feathers or a few cotton balls
Prize or prizes

Though this game is liveliest when played with a feather, a feather of any useful size can be hard to find. And cotton balls work almost as well.

Guests are lined up in two groups at one end of the room. The object is to carry the feather, or cotton balls, by spoon across the room to an arbitrary point and back again without losing the cargo. If the feather falls, the player must retrieve it using the spoon only.

At the command, "Go!" the race begins, with the first two players carrying their spoons and racing each other across the room and back. The spoon is then handed off to the next in line until all have done it.

At first glance the game appears simple, but participants learn quickly that speed creates wind—and wind causes havoc. Moving gracefully and slowly turns out to be the key.

The first team to finish gets some kind of reward.

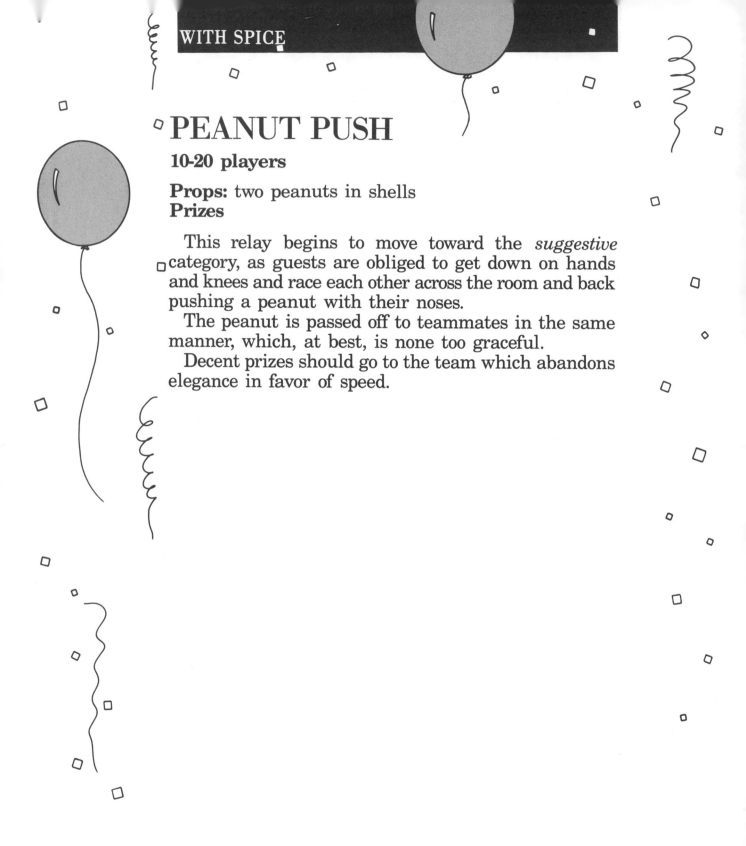

PEANUT PUSH

10-20 players

Props: two peanuts in shells
Prizes

This relay begins to move toward the *suggestive* category, as guests are obliged to get down on hands and knees and race each other across the room and back pushing a peanut with their noses.

The peanut is passed off to teammates in the same manner, which, at best, is none too graceful.

Decent prizes should go to the team which abandons elegance in favor of speed.

MUSICAL LAPS

8-20 couples

Props: music from the radio, piano or tape player, chairs (enough for half the crowd less two)

A variation of musical chairs, this game is a sexier version. Chairs are placed in a circle, and when the music starts, men walk one way inside the circle, and ladies walk the other way outside.

When the music stops, men rush for the chairs and women jump into their laps. With one chair removed each round, couples are eliminated progressively.

The game goes on until only one aggressive couple is left.

Outlasting the crowd is its own reward.

BODY-TO-BODY

6-15 couples

Props: two oranges or two carrots or 2 Lifesavers and plenty of toothpicks or 2 cigarette papers (roll your own variety)

The advent of any of these relays will convice a fair number of guests that "they're getting into the good stuff."

The group is divided into two teams, as always, except here it's necessary to alternate the men and women, and known couples aren't allowed to stand next to each other. Without this rule these relays are pointless.

Each relay is basically the same, the object being to pass the item in question from one end of the line to the other, with the fastest team being winners and nobody really caring who's fastest.

Each item is passed differently. The orange is placed in the crook of the neck, held by chin and shoulder and passed without hands to the next player in line.

The toothpick is held between the lips with the Lifesaver hanging on it, then maneuvered onto the toothpick protruding from the next pair of lips. This is not as easy as it sounds. The hostess can either explain, or guests can discover, that it's necessary to keep the toothpick tilted upward when receiving the Lifesaver, to prevent the little disc sliding off, and a good idea to tilt the toothpick downward when passing it on to someone else. All that toothpick tilting is tricky and distracting when you're less than an inch from someone else's lips!

The cigarette paper is kept against the nose by inhalation and passed to the next nose—somehow!

And the carrot—here it comes—goes from one pair of knees to another . . . and nobody can say *that's* not suggestive!

If anything falls to the ground, players are supposed to retrieve the item without hands, which they generally can't do, so they cheat.

A variant of this game—not exactly a relay, but a race to the finish, nevertheless—involves balloons which are only partially blown up and have a rather saggy appearance. The balloons are given to all the men on both teams, and at the call of "Go!" the men turn to the women nearest them, and by placing the balloons between their two bodies, the couple tries to hug the balloon to death . . . until it pops or they give up out of embarrassment.

The winning team is, of course, the first to pop all the balloons—which may or may not ever happen.

This feels like an x-rated game when you're playing it, but since we did all that hugging in our church social hall it presumably has an ecumenical stamp of approval.

One or two such games in an evening and you've had your guests lip-to-lip, chest-to-chest, and hip-to-hip, and some of your more inhibited guests should go home feeling they've had a great time.

CARNAL KNOWLEDGE

5-15 couples

Props: one blindfold and enough chairs for all the women

Here's another high pulse game. Men are sent out of the room, while the women climb onto the chairs and pull up skirt or pant leg to reveal their calves.

The host then blindfolds one of the men and leads him into the room. The man is moved from woman to woman, and feeling her lower legs, he tries to determine who she is. Surprisingly, a great many men will miss their own wives—as they discover once the blindfold is removed.

The rest of the men are brought in one by one, and the game goes on. Men are asked to identify their choices out loud, providing entertainment for spectators as well as participants.

Sometimes guests will opt to play the game in reverse, with women feeling the legs of the men.

Another game where the doing is its own reward.

STOCKING-GRAPEFRUIT RELAY

10-20 players

Props: two belts, two nylon stockings, two grapefruit, two small rubber balls

This is a relay which defies categorization. The visual effect is funny—some would say "gross."

In preparation, the host drops a grapefruit down into the toe of a nylon stocking, then ties the open end of the stocking securely to a belt.

Guests are divided into two teams standing at one end of the room. The lead player on each team puts on the belt, letting the grapefruit-in-stocking hang down between his legs. (Not exactly lovely looking.)

The rubber ball is placed at the starting line, and by maneuvering his hips, the player gets the stocking swinging and hopefully connects with the ball. The purpose is to bat the ball down to a prescribed goal and back again without hands or feet!

It is almost embarrassing watching this game in action. Players appear to have sprouted a long and ugly tail, and the accompanying hip movements add humor and a touch of obscenity. But we've seen it played in church crowds so it's obviously not on the banned list.

HIDDEN WORDS PUZZLE

10-40 players

Props: Copies of the "Hidden Words" game (one per player) and pencils
Prizes

Guests are given sheets with what, at first glance, appears to be a square filled with random letters. The host announces that hidden among the letters are words pertaining to babies (or whatever the theme happens to be). On the count of "Go!" guests will have ten minutes to find the hidden words and circle them, and the guest with the longest list wins a prize. All words are made up of consecutive letters, though some words are diagonal, some run from bottom to top and others from right to left.

It's important for the host to keep in mind, when making up an alternative "Hidden Words" game for a theme other than the baby-shower game included here, that after the desired words are put into the square, the remaining blanks should consist mostly of consonants. Vowels tend to create extra, unwanted words.

The example given has 15 words pertaining to babies—which seems to be about the maximum one can fit into a square 15 by 15.

```
S T E I H L M E X T E B N Q M
E X M A S T B A B Y Y G U U C
T O N S M O N F U N A I S R A
Y B O T T L E M N S L F T E P
A V P R E G N A N T B T A A O
D T O O E A R N Y K O S N T W
H F A L T G I R L I Y U Q T D
T G E L H B D I A P E R O U E
R B M E I T M P C N R M Y S R
I D O R N P A L S R Y C O B L
B A T H G O B O E S Y D E M I
W G H X T I N H S N N I M A B
J N E A R A T T L E Q T S O E
S O R C R A W L O U D U U D A
P R Y F A M I L Y S H O W E R
```

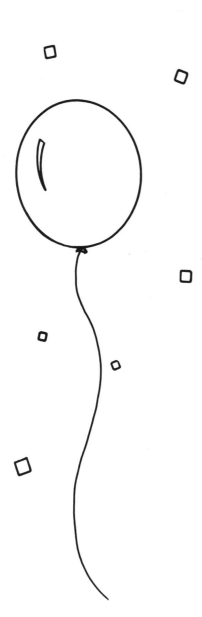

CHAPTER 6

THEME GAMES

Although the games in this category are fine for any kind of party, they are particularly useful for parties with a purpose—such as wedding or baby showers, anniversaries and various fund-raising parties.

Some of the games are ready to play "as is" and others can be easily adapted to the theme.

When more than two games are planned for such a party, it's best if one of the games is something entirely different so guests won't feel they're inundated by the theme.

LAPEL SECRETS

10-50 players

Props: small items (such as a safety pin, label or tag) which can be concealed beneath a man's lapel (see list and instruction sheet), instruction sheets and pencils

Similar to *Body Search*, this mixer varies in that nobody knows how many of the concealed items exist because the host decides. This means that every male guest is subject to be searched by everyone else.

The item hidden beneath the lapel should have some relevance to the theme of the party. A fund-raiser for the Heart Association, for instance, might involve tiny hearts under the lapels, while a Little League affair might call for small wooden bats.

As soon as most of the guests have arrived, the group is invited to begin searching for the hidden objects. The prize goes to the first person who lists the names of every man involved.

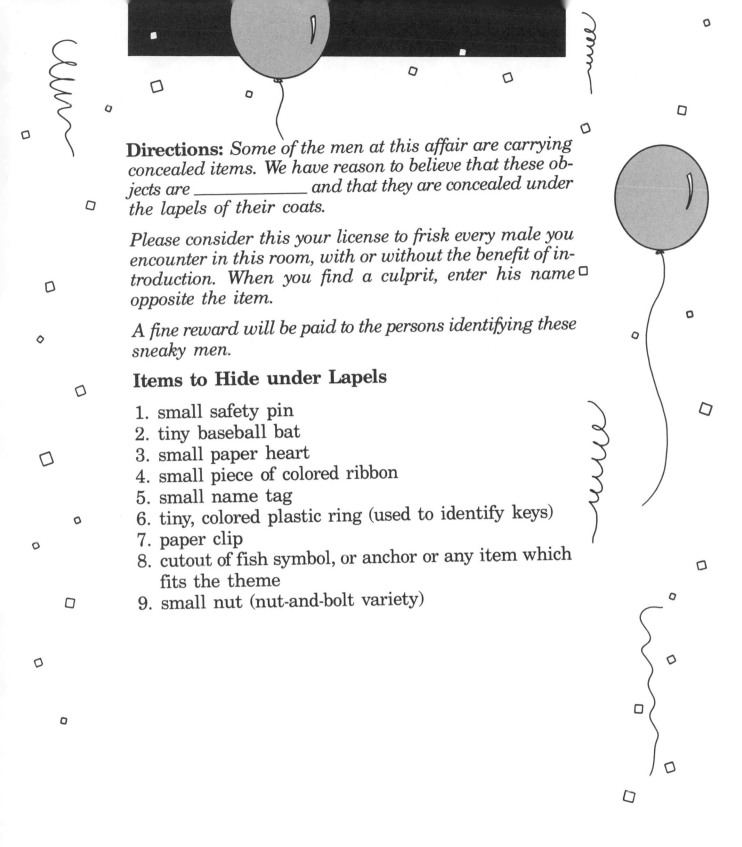

Directions: *Some of the men at this affair are carrying concealed items. We have reason to believe that these objects are _____ and that they are concealed under the lapels of their coats.*

Please consider this your license to frisk every male you encounter in this room, with or without the benefit of introduction. When you find a culprit, enter his name opposite the item.

A fine reward will be paid to the persons identifying these sneaky men.

Items to Hide under Lapels

1. small safety pin
2. tiny baseball bat
3. small paper heart
4. small piece of colored ribbon
5. small name tag
6. tiny, colored plastic ring (used to identify keys)
7. paper clip
8. cutout of fish symbol, or anchor or any item which fits the theme
9. small nut (nut-and-bolt variety)

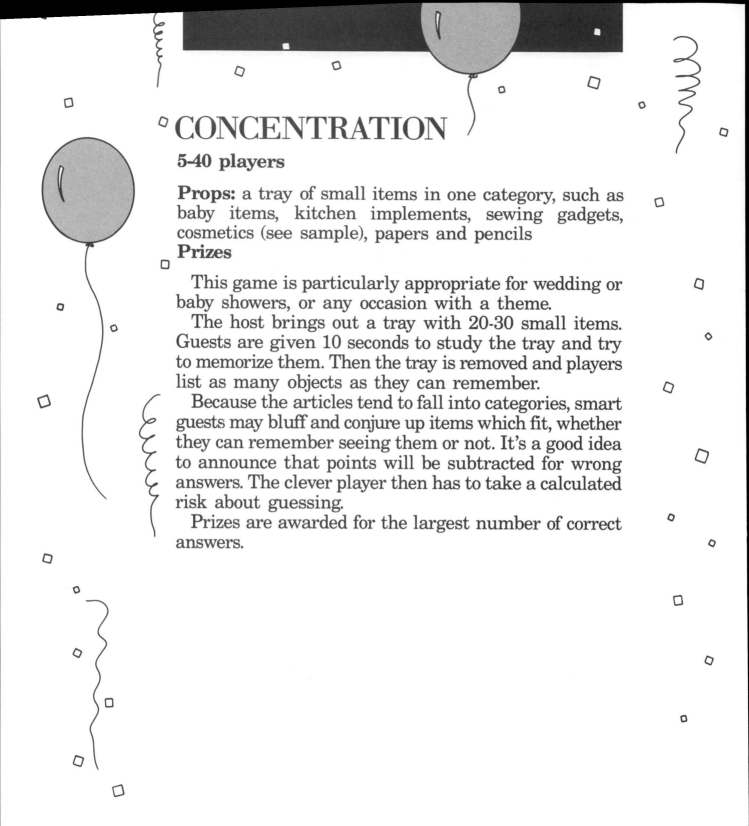

CONCENTRATION

5-40 players

Props: a tray of small items in one category, such as baby items, kitchen implements, sewing gadgets, cosmetics (see sample), papers and pencils
Prizes

This game is particularly appropriate for wedding or baby showers, or any occasion with a theme.

The host brings out a tray with 20-30 small items. Guests are given 10 seconds to study the tray and try to memorize them. Then the tray is removed and players list as many objects as they can remember.

Because the articles tend to fall into categories, smart guests may bluff and conjure up items which fit, whether they can remember seeing them or not. It's a good idea to announce that points will be subtracted for wrong answers. The clever player then has to take a calculated risk about guessing.

Prizes are awarded for the largest number of correct answers.

Suggested Items

Baby Items

diaper
rattle
nipple
jar of baby food
washcloth
bib
feeding spoon
rubber pants
bottle brush
baby cup
cotton swabs
rubber ball
teething ring
diaper pins
baby bottle
pacifier
baby hairbrush
baby shoe
tiny comb
baby dish
petroleum jelly
hair bow
can of formula
cotton balls
stuffed animal
talcum powder

Kitchen Items

spoon
dishrag
small pot lid
glass
cork
corkscrew
jar lid
bottle opener
fork
cup
rolling pin
recipe card
bar of soap
vanilla
pencil
thumbtack
tea strainer
birthday candle
small pot
paring knife
eggbeater
paper muffin cup
toothpick
salad plate

Cosmetics

lipstick
hairbrush
bar of soap
eyebrow pencil
necklace
liquid makeup
hairpin
razor
nail scissors
nail polish
face cream
eyeliner
deodorant
lipstick brush
comb
cotton swab
eye shadow
tweezers
earring
mascara
hair dryer
vitamin
emery board
perfume
bath powder
face powder
facial brush
eye shadow

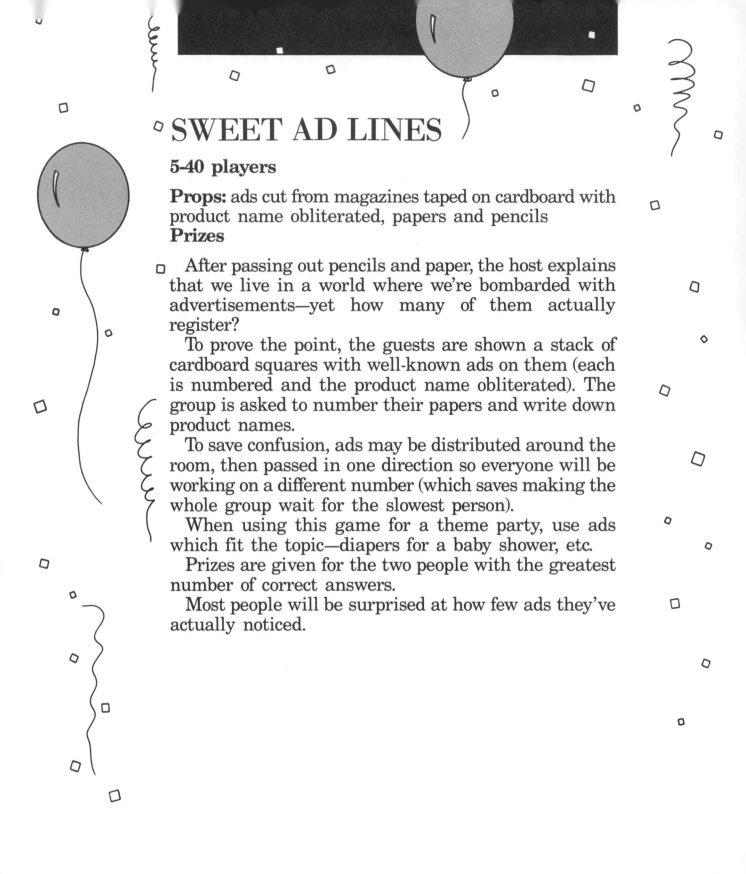

SWEET AD LINES

5-40 players

Props: ads cut from magazines taped on cardboard with product name obliterated, papers and pencils
Prizes

After passing out pencils and paper, the host explains that we live in a world where we're bombarded with advertisements—yet how many of them actually register?

To prove the point, the guests are shown a stack of cardboard squares with well-known ads on them (each is numbered and the product name obliterated). The group is asked to number their papers and write down product names.

To save confusion, ads may be distributed around the room, then passed in one direction so everyone will be working on a different number (which saves making the whole group wait for the slowest person).

When using this game for a theme party, use ads which fit the topic—diapers for a baby shower, etc.

Prizes are given for the two people with the greatest number of correct answers.

Most people will be surprised at how few ads they've actually noticed.

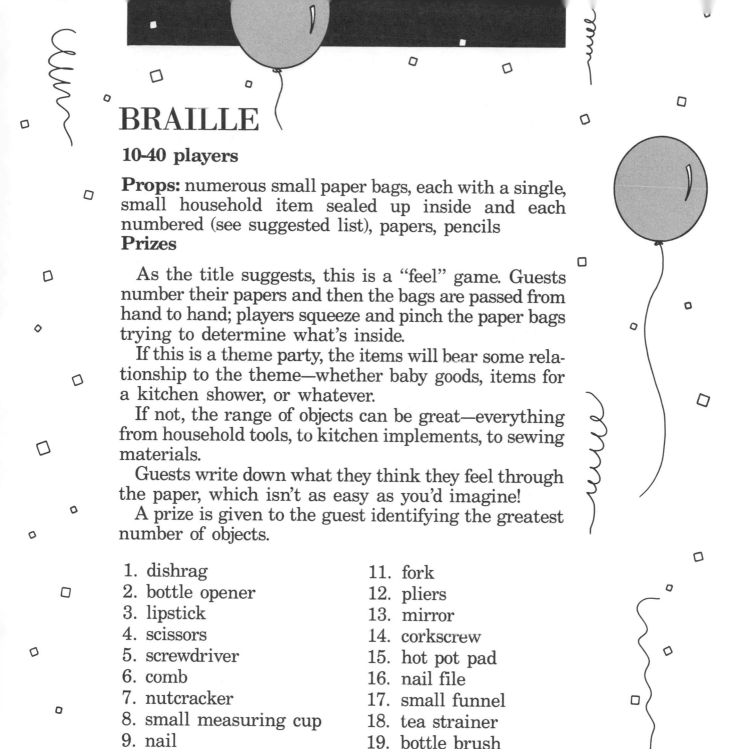

BRAILLE

10-40 players

Props: numerous small paper bags, each with a single, small household item sealed up inside and each numbered (see suggested list), papers, pencils
Prizes

As the title suggests, this is a "feel" game. Guests number their papers and then the bags are passed from hand to hand; players squeeze and pinch the paper bags trying to determine what's inside.

If this is a theme party, the items will bear some relationship to the theme—whether baby goods, items for a kitchen shower, or whatever.

If not, the range of objects can be great—everything from household tools, to kitchen implements, to sewing materials.

Guests write down what they think they feel through the paper, which isn't as easy as you'd imagine!

A prize is given to the guest identifying the greatest number of objects.

1. dishrag
2. bottle opener
3. lipstick
4. scissors
5. screwdriver
6. comb
7. nutcracker
8. small measuring cup
9. nail
10. spoon
11. fork
12. pliers
13. mirror
14. corkscrew
15. hot pot pad
16. nail file
17. small funnel
18. tea strainer
19. bottle brush
20. ballpoint pen

CAVE LANGUAGE

5-30 players

Props: sheets with clues and blank words (see sample), pencils
Prize or prizes

This is a speed game in which players using a clue word race each other to figure out the code, and then additional words.

The host shows a mysterious sample of ancient writing found in a cave. The sample includes one word translated into today's language, but all the rest of the words remain a mystery. Guests are asked to help translate the rest of the text, which the host has been told, deals with recreation, both ancient and modern.

Please note that although the sample game centers on recreational activities, the host may use the supplied code to make up alternative games which fit a theme party.

This game is especially appreciated by guests with a penchant for logical deduction.

Directions: *Using the sample word below, figure out the rest of the words. All of them have to do with recreation.*

G O L F

A B C D E F G H I J K L M

N O P Q R S T U V W X Y Z

FOOTBALL FACTS

5 players

Props: one *Football Fantasy* quiz sheet for each five people (see sample), pencils
Prizes

While the following football quiz is designed for avid sports buffs and can be used at any sports-related party, such as a party given on Superbowl Sunday, similar quizzes can be designed around other themes by anyone with access to an encyclopedia.

The object of this quiz is to fill in the twenty-eight blanks with the names of the twenty-eight NFL football teams, using the rather tricky definitions as clues.

Prizes can be given the first team to finish the task.

There are 28 NFL teams. Using the definitions, name both the team and its city.

1. Flag wavers _____
2. Long-legged runabouts ____
3. Bucking beasts _____
4. Heavenly beings _____
5. Plenty sunburned _____
6. Waterfowl _____
7. Patched eyes _____
8. Striped and mean _____
9. Abound on the savannah __
10. Head honchos _____
11. High voltage _____
12. High in the priesthood ____
13. 'n Indians _____
14. Battering . . . _____

15. Gullivers _____
16. Gold diggers _____
17. Stuffed teddys _____
18. Supersonics _____
19. Thieves of the Lost Ark ____
20. Ironmen _____
21. Chocolate lovers _____
22. Foldin' money _____
23. Boxers _____
24. Flipper _____
25. Heavily taloned _____
26. "Texas tea" _____
27. Norsemen _____
28. Bald birds _____

Football Cities

Los Angeles
San Diego
San Francisco
Seattle
Chicago
New York (2)
Kansas City
Indianapolis
Atlanta

Minnesota
Detroit
Denver
New Orleans
Washington
Cincinnati
New England
Cleveland
Houston

Pittsburgh
Green Bay
Dallas
Los Angeles
Tampa Bay
Buffalo
Miami
Philadelphia
St. Louis

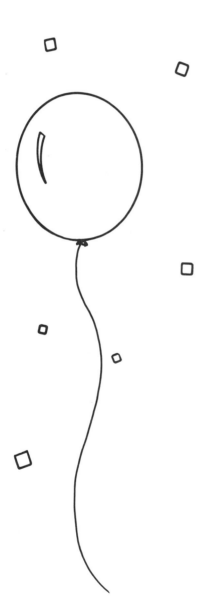

CHAPTER 7

MISCELLANEOUS GAMES

These games cannot be neatly categorized. In fact, some are *events* rather than games. But all are proven winners for parties.

PHOTO FINISH

16-40 players

Props: copies of *Photo Finish* game (2 per team), one instant camera per team
Prizes

This game stands alone as both unusual and entertaining. Few games call on so much ingenuity from guests. It's got the built-in challenge of a car rally, but it's lots more fun. *Photo Finish* will really stick in your guests' memories.

By way of preparation, the host calls guests in advance and asks them to bring instant cameras, making sure that there will be one camera per team.

Once all the guests arrive, teams are formed, with each team consisting of 5 people (enough to fit into one car). The object is for the teams to spend an hour photographing the suggested events and activities—choosing carefully as they weigh their options: Should they go for the more difficult shots that involve higher point values, or aim for a completed task with lesser points? Or should they give up a shot or two to earn extra points by being the first team home?

How imaginative should they try to be? One group we know of won the prize by finding a laundromat and having themselves photographed *inside* the clothes dryer.

A prize goes to the team with the most points. New wrinkles can be added to the game by having the group vote on not only the most unique picture, but also the funniest or the most artistic. As a final touch the host can have all the best pictures made into a collage.

Directions: *You are to take pictures of your team doing any of the listed items. Only 8 shots per team will be counted, so choose your pictures wisely. You have ONE HOUR from the time you leave the house. (A team that does not have film receives an additional 5 minutes to buy film.)*

	Point Value
Team members in a telephone booth (the real kind)	3 points
All team members blowing bubbles (new gum is best)	3 points
The team standing next to a statue	4 points
Everyone afloat in a boat (with or without any water)	4 points
Everyone adoring a new Cadillac (with price sticker attached)	3 points
Someone on your team holding a frog	4 points
Team choice picture, points go to "Most Imaginative" (by popular vote)	6 points
The team on a diving board (extra point for each member wearing a bathing suit)	4 points
The bunch of you dancing around a fireplug	3 points
One member of the team astride a police motorcycle	5 points
Shaking hands with a Marine in uniform (an alternate—team with a Marine on guard duty)	4 points
Someone on the team riding a horse	4 points
The first team home!	6 points

REMEMBER TO DRIVE CAREFULLY — *HIGH SCORE* IS THE WINNER

MYSTERY MENU

15-50 players

Props: typed and photocopied menu for each guest (see sample), numerous dinner items: salads, one or two meat dishes, two desserts, one or two vegetables, plus single items such as toothpicks, carrot sticks, olives, wine (food items listed on sample menu)

Mystery Menu is a dinner game which takes the whole evening and as such, it's not so much a game, as an event!

We've given, or been guests at, this party on at least half a dozen occasions and each time it was a success. It seems to fit all ages and all seasons and pleases everyone who likes to eat!

Preparations for the dinner are greater than normal and the dinner itself requires extra couples to help serve—at least one person for every four people seated in the dining room. In spite of all the work, the party is interesting enough for everyone, hosts included, to make it worth the effort.

Menus must be reproduced ahead of time and the food laid out in the kitchen systematically so your waiter-friends can find it quickly. It's best to put signs or labels near each serving dish #1, #2, so that the servers refer to numbers rather than stopping to translate from their menus.

Guests have been invited to what seems an ordinary dinner. But when it's time to sit down they notice the table seems rather scantily set—centerpiece and place mats and little else.

As they wait expectantly for their food, the hostess comes in with menus and guests are asked to study them and then select three items for their first course.

People realize quickly that these are peculiar menus. Everything is in code. For instance, *crystal cascade* could mean water, or ice cream, or who knows what. *Field pickins* could be salad, potatoes, or a vegetable. (Code names should have some vague relationship to the food they represent.)

After giving guests a brief time with the menu, the hosts and helpers come in with pads and pencils and take down guests' orders—leaving them in the dark as to what, exactly, they've ordered.

The surprise comes when diners discover that everything to be served—from napkins, to silverware, to dessert—is on the menu and part of the code.

One guest may find he's ordered a napkin, a spoon, and a toothpick as a first course, but no food, whereas another may unknowingly order salad, ice cream and spaghetti, but no utensils.

Guests are directed to make do with what they get, which may mean resorting to fingers.

Menus are removed between courses, then brought back for successive rounds. As the meal goes on, guests invariably compare notes and become wise to their orders, though there are always those who forget what they ordered earlier and find themselves with repeat items.

Throughout dinner, there's never a problem with conversation lagging. This meal gives everyone plenty to talk about!

At the end it's wise to let the guests have whatever they've missed . . . if they're not too full!

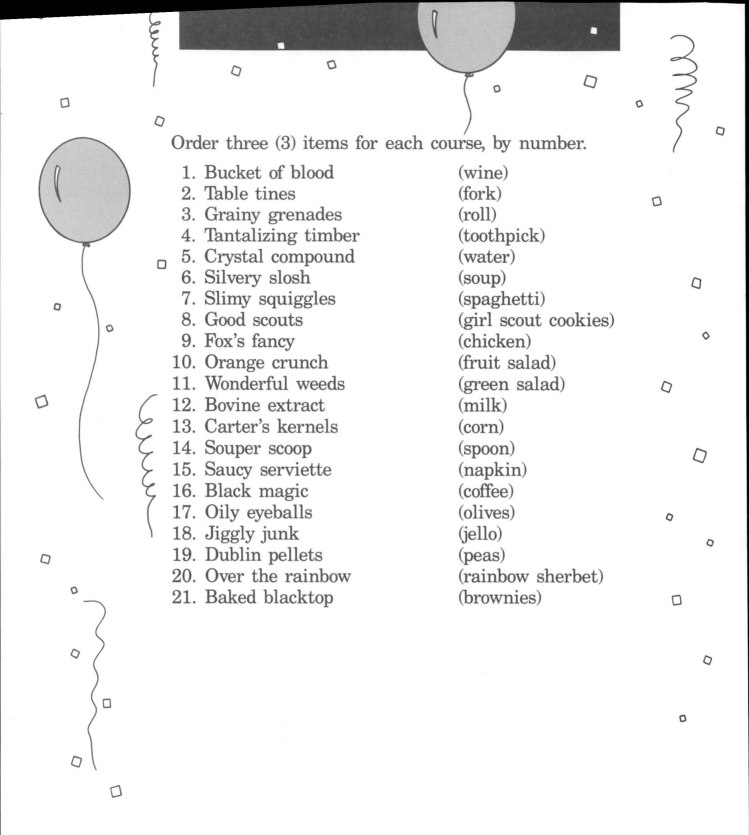

Order three (3) items for each course, by number.

1. Bucket of blood   (wine)
2. Table tines   (fork)
3. Grainy grenades   (roll)
4. Tantalizing timber   (toothpick)
5. Crystal compound   (water)
6. Silvery slosh   (soup)
7. Slimy squiggles   (spaghetti)
8. Good scouts   (girl scout cookies)
9. Fox's fancy   (chicken)
10. Orange crunch   (fruit salad)
11. Wonderful weeds   (green salad)
12. Bovine extract   (milk)
13. Carter's kernels   (corn)
14. Souper scoop   (spoon)
15. Saucy serviette   (napkin)
16. Black magic   (coffee)
17. Oily eyeballs   (olives)
18. Jiggly junk   (jello)
19. Dublin pellets   (peas)
20. Over the rainbow   (rainbow sherbet)
21. Baked blacktop   (brownies)

PARTY PING PONG

9-20 players

Props: ping-pong table or tables, paddles, balls

Handicap tennis is usually easier to arrange than party ping-pong—for the reason that while tennis players tend to have access to several courts, few people can scare up more than one ping-pong table. Which leaves the problem of how to keep nonplaying guests occupied.

The most workable format for party ping-pong is some sort of round-robin, where guests alternate playing doubles with a variety of partners.

The host can arrange the pairings in advance, giving each player a chance to play both with people at the same level and with those better or worse.

Round one, for instance, might pit players A and B (both experts) against each other, with players C and D (novices) as their partners. But another round would be reserved for four players who are *all* experts.

Individual scores would be kept for all rounds and the player with the highest cumulative total declared the winner.

If less serious ping-pong is desired, variations can be introduced. An entertaining alternative involves four players who take turns hitting the ball once, laying their paddles down, then racing to the far end of the table to pick up a loose paddle and prepare to hit the ball again. Players are responsible for every other shot at each end of the table.

Needless to say, the whole thing is a madhouse. Not only do players forget to leave their paddles behind, they also forget to run, and sometimes they forget to hit the ball!

Team points are scored every time either of one's opponents misses, which happens rather more frequently in this game than usual.

But it's a rip-roaring version of ping-pong and lots of exercise. And those who aren't playing can stand by and laugh!

153

VARIATIONS ON THE DANCE

10 or more players

Props: cornmeal, a broom, dance cards

A dance as part of a party has the potential for being either a great success or a resounding flop. Dances are best not tried with groups unless the host knows for certain that most of the people are with partners, or can find them within the group, and also that most feel inclined to dance. It is a guaranteed failure to have too loud music (so that nondancers can't talk) and only a small percentage of the guests dancing. After a short session of this, the hosts will look up and find a lot of people gone.

But in a party of youngish people in a home where there's enough space for nondancers to escape the music, dancing can be a boon. We've put the dancing out on our cement turn-around area behind the garage, and we've used D.J.s and live bands (mariachi, Calypso and Reggae) and for us the dancing has worked. All that's needed aside from music is clean cement and a lot of corn-meal to spread around.

Our party philosophy of total group involvement works on the dance floor as everywhere else. We never leave the dancing entirely to chance; eventually we try to involve everyone. The single best "involver" is the *snowball dance,* for which you have to have the cooperation of whoever is providing the music. In the *snowball,* one couple dances alone for a short period, after which the music stops and those two go out and find two other partners. At the next pause in the music, the four locate four more, and so on, until everyone within sight is out on the dance floor. The *snowball* is beautifully non-discriminatory. Shorties end up with tallies, young men with older women, grandmothers with boys, and always because "everyone's doing it," so it's okay. We've found the *snowball dance* generates more good will and real involvement than any dance mixer we've seen in action.

Another good dance mixer—a real oldie—is the *broom dance*. As couples begin dancing, some solo man is handed a broom and he must go out on the dance floor and hand off his broom to somebody else; he takes the woman and the other man gets the broom. Most men will get into the spirit of the thing and keep the broom circulating throughout that dance.

An announcement by the music provider, *Women's Choice*, seems to give shyer women the freedom to go ask a man to dance, a nice reversal of roles. Believe it or not, there are still women out there who find it hard to be the aggressor in such matters. It's easier when everyone's doing it.

For parties where a large part of the evening will be spent dancing, women can be given dance cards for selected dances. Before the dancing starts they can invite men to sign their cards—another way to overcome feminine reserve and insure a reasonable supply of partners.

A final note about dance music: When your party is a "theme" party and special dance music is provided, such as Calypso or Reggae, it doesn't seem to matter as much whether people dance. Theme music becomes entertainment and those who sit out feel comfortable doing so.

DUCK SOUP

5-50 players

Props: one copy of the *Duck Soup* game for every six or seven people (see sample), pencils

This game has been very popular with our guests over the years. It's a food-oriented quiz, and not only does it prove the great variety of food-related expressions in our society, it also spans the generations; some food-based expressions which were in vogue in the forties and fifties are almost unknown to the young adults of today. For this reason the game is best played in teams.

After dividing the crowd into groups, with no more than six or seven to a group, the host puts each group in a different area of the house with a pencil and a copy of the game. At the call of "Start," the various groups begin filling in the blanks.

If each contingent is lucky enough to have players spanning the age ranges, you'll see a lot of appreciation expressed during this game. Older people come into their own by knowing the expression "cheesecake," whereas younger players may be better acquainted with the term for an argument between ball players and an umpire, a "rhubarb."

The game ends when one group completes the quiz or when "time" is called.

With everyone assembled, the host goes over the questions one by one, letting guests supply the correct answers.

As is so often the case with a game which involves a lot of team spirit, interest in this one remains high right through the denouement!

QUIZ

1. When you're embarrassed, you turn red as a _____.
2. A crowded bus packs the riders in like _____.
3. A person or thing that's worthless isn't worth a hill of _____.
4. An actor who's always acting, even offstage, is a _____.
5. If you're really smart, you know your _____.
6. An intelligent person is also a smart _____.
7. An unexpected bonus is a _____.
8. A runt is a _____.
9. If you really like something you go _____ over it.
10. One who's a grouchy meany is often called a _____.
11. A person not easily aroused is cool as a _____.
12. If you've pulverized something, you've made _____ of it.
13. An old-fashioned joke is usually pure _____.
14. If you've heard it six times, it's an old _____.
15. Something too dangerous to get involved with is a hot _____.
16. Someone more than a little wacky is nutty as a _____.
17. Folding money is called _____.
18. Anyone who is afraid is just plain _____.
19. Hamburgers, they say, are as American as _____.
20. If you're good at what you do you're really worth your _____.

21. New York City is known as the Big _____.
22. When you don't care about it, you don't give a _____.
23. Something quite simple is as easy as _____.
24. An attractive girl can be considered a real _____.
25. She might also be labeled a real _____.
26. And an appealing photo of an appealing young woman is ____.
27. If mum's the word, you had better _____.
28. If you can't hold on to anything, you're a _____ fingers.
29. You don't believe it? Then say it's a lot of _____.
30. If you're in deep trouble, your _____ is cooked.
31. What sits on top of your neck is known as your _____.
32. When your new car stalls for the 90th time, you've got a ____.
33. Sit on your hat and you squash it flat as a _____.
34. A flop on Broadway is a play judged a _____.
35. Archie Bunker's favorite criticism is a sound called a _____.
36. When the players and the ump go at it, they have a _____.
37. Fog so thick you can slice it is called _____.
38. Zero is a big _____.
39. Earn a living, and you bring home the _____.
40. You got all these expressions right? Holy _____.

HANDICAP TENNIS

8-20 players

Props: tennis court for every 4 people, various handicapping implements (see samples), two large posterboard charts

An afternoon or early evening of tennis turns into a party when the host prearranges the matches so that everyone is handicapped a little and the really good players handicapped a lot.

All kinds of devices and implements can be used: whistles, bells, tin cups of water, ping-pong rackets, umbrellas, raincoats, funny hats (especially those which tend to fly off during a point), broken-arm slings, ski mittens, grass skirts, neckties.

It takes a tennis player to arrange this. Any reasonably good player will recognize the degree of handicapping of each of these devices—from the raincoat worn by the fairly poor player to the ping-pong paddle assigned to the excellent player.

Handicapping is limited only by the host's imagination. Players can be required to run holding a cup of water, to ring a bell before every contact with the ball, to play lefthanded, to blow a whistle between shots.

The handicapping will usually require some monitoring by the host. Somebody has to make sure the sneakier players don't cheat.

And it helps if all pairings and games are spelled out explicitly on a large posterboard. For example, *Round one: Dave and Mary vs. Bill and Joan. Harry and Sally vs. Bob and Sandra. Play 7 games, no-ad.*

Rounds 2 and 3 will have different pairings and perhaps a different number of total games played.

The day will be more interesting if men and women keep their partners, while varying their opponents, with prizes given to the winning couple.

Also, the smart host will try to match up teams and handicaps so everyone has an equal chance of winning.

159

HANDICAPS

1. small dinner bell (ring after hitting ball)
2. referee's whistle (blow before hitting ball)
3. measuring cup full of water (carry during play—lose the point if any spills!)
4. raincoat (wear over tennis clothes)
5. boxing glove (wear on racket hand)
6. ping-pong racket (use instead of racket)
7. funny hat (or hats . . . preferably floppy)
8. ski gloves (wear on both hands)
9. grass skirt (man wears over tennis shorts)
10. galoshes (wear over, or instead of, tennis shoes)
11. broken-arm sling (wear on nondominant arm)
12. necktie (wear over tennis shirt)
13. play lefthanded (excellent player only)
14. umbrella (carry during play)
15. let ball bounce before every shot—even at net

ANSWERS TO QUIZZES

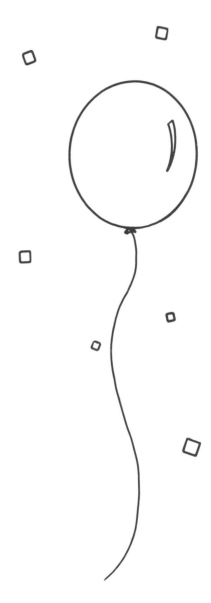

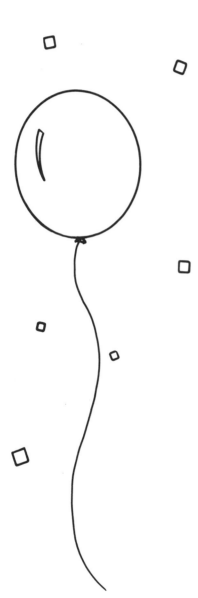

Answers to Rounded Brain Quiz
From page 77

1. German train station
2. $2 + 2 = 5$
3. Brahms, Beethoven, Bach, Hayden, Mozart, Mendelssohn, Mahler, Schumann
4. The speed of a falling object
5. Large, primitive bird
6. After dinner
7. Disruption of body's physiological clock
8. Change in sound wave's frequency (pitch) as it moves
9. Words that sound like what they represent
10. Comes from Italian, "Banca Erupta," or "broken table"—(angry creditors broke moneylenders' tables)
11. In the Indian Ocean, east of Africa
12. Gorilla, chimpanzee, orangutan, gibbon
13. First and second vertabrae
14. A plant leans toward the source of light
15. A mixture is a mechanical mix, a chemical is bonded chemically
16. Aspirin
17. Extra vigor as a result of cross-breeding
18. Health, love, money and the time to enjoy them
19. The area between the latitudes known as the Tropic of Cancer and the Tropic of Capricorn
20. A pen name
21. Archimedes
22. The coccyx
23. The stalactite grows from the top down—the stalagmite from the bottom up
24. Cumulonimbus
25. Roberta Flack

163

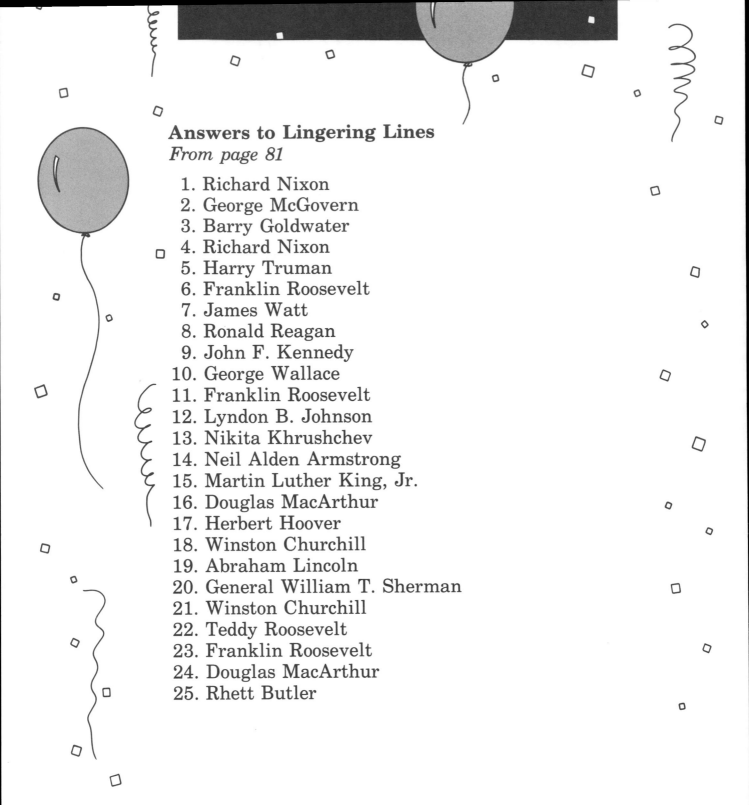

Answers to Lingering Lines
From page 81

1. Richard Nixon
2. George McGovern
3. Barry Goldwater
4. Richard Nixon
5. Harry Truman
6. Franklin Roosevelt
7. James Watt
8. Ronald Reagan
9. John F. Kennedy
10. George Wallace
11. Franklin Roosevelt
12. Lyndon B. Johnson
13. Nikita Khrushchev
14. Neil Alden Armstrong
15. Martin Luther King, Jr.
16. Douglas MacArthur
17. Herbert Hoover
18. Winston Churchill
19. Abraham Lincoln
20. General William T. Sherman
21. Winston Churchill
22. Teddy Roosevelt
23. Franklin Roosevelt
24. Douglas MacArthur
25. Rhett Butler

Answers to RVW General Knowledge Test
From page 88 & 89

1. Alan Lerner and Frederick Lowe
2. Medical condition— inadequate blood flow
3. P.T. Barnum
4. Ayn Rand
5. K2—in Kashmir
6. Rita Coolidge
7. Emily Bronte
8. Mexico City
9. Nothing by mouth
10. 1789
11. Charles Darwin
12. Sullivan
13. Joseph Lister
14. William Styron
15. A cave explorer
16. George Orwell
17. Consumption (tuberculosis)
18. Sweet, sour, salty, bitter
19. Purchase of Alaska
20. Stephen Foster
21. Nine
22. Emily Dickinson
23. T.S. Eliot
24. Twelve

25. Lawyer
26. Jonathan Swift
27. Doctrine of mutual protection among nations of the Western Hemisphere
28. 7—Munich, 1972
29. Lieut. Pinkerton
30. Navy
31. British revolutionary anarchist and folk hero
32. Aldous Huxley
33. Rapid Eye Movements
34. As needed—medical charting instruction
35. Doc Blanchard & Glenn Davis, All-Americans at Army during the 40's.
36. Nathaniel Hawthorne
37. H.L. Mencken
38. "First do no harm"— medical term
39. Lecturer or guide

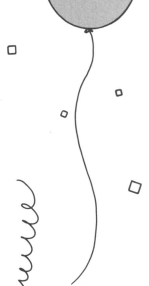

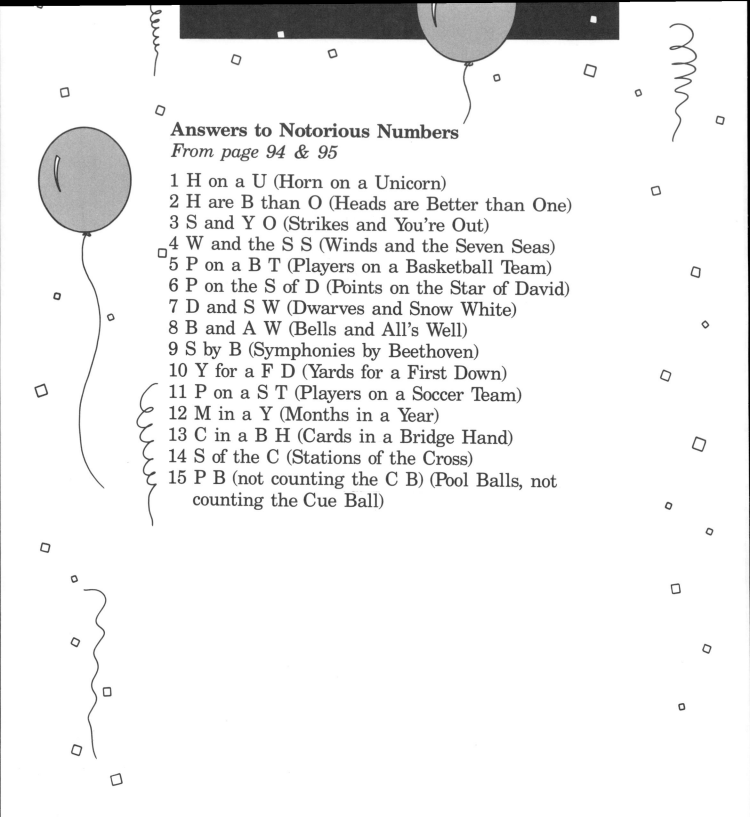

Answers to Notorious Numbers
From page 94 & 95

1 H on a U (Horn on a Unicorn)
2 H are B than O (Heads are Better than One)
3 S and Y O (Strikes and You're Out)
4 W and the S S (Winds and the Seven Seas)
5 P on a B T (Players on a Basketball Team)
6 P on the S of D (Points on the Star of David)
7 D and S W (Dwarves and Snow White)
8 B and A W (Bells and All's Well)
9 S by B (Symphonies by Beethoven)
10 Y for a F D (Yards for a First Down)
11 P on a S T (Players on a Soccer Team)
12 M in a Y (Months in a Year)
13 C in a B H (Cards in a Bridge Hand)
14 S of the C (Stations of the Cross)
15 P B (not counting the C B) (Pool Balls, not counting the Cue Ball)

16 O in a P (Ounces in a Pound)

17 Y L (Year Locusts)

18 Y O to V (Years Old to Vote)

19th H of a G C (Hole of a Golf Course)

20 C in a P (Cigarettes in a Pack)

21 G S (Gun Salute)

26 M in a M (Miles in a Marathon)

30 D hath S, A, J, and N (Days hath September, April, June and November)

32 T in the M (Teeth in the Mouth)

40 T and A B (Theives and Ali Baba)

50 S in the U (States in the Union)

60 S in a M (Seconds in a Minute)

100 C in a D (Cents in a Dollar)

101 D (Dalmations)

212 D at which W B (Degrees at which Water Boils)

360 D in a C (Degrees in a Circle)

5280 F in a M (Feet in a Mile)

25,000 M around the E (Miles around the Equator)

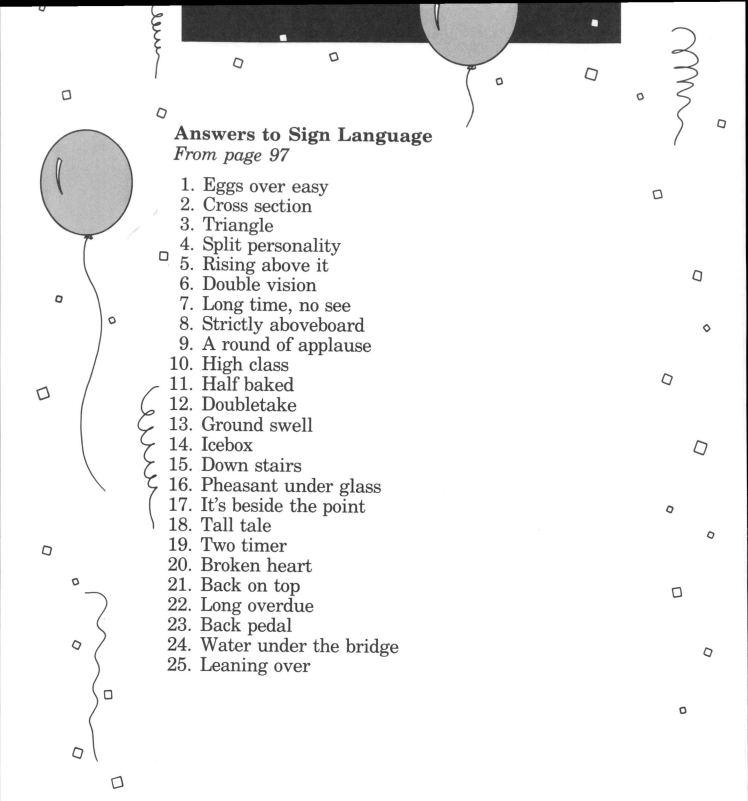

Answers to Sign Language
From page 97

1. Eggs over easy
2. Cross section
3. Triangle
4. Split personality
5. Rising above it
6. Double vision
7. Long time, no see
8. Strictly aboveboard
9. A round of applause
10. High class
11. Half baked
12. Doubletake
13. Ground swell
14. Icebox
15. Down stairs
16. Pheasant under glass
17. It's beside the point
18. Tall tale
19. Two timer
20. Broken heart
21. Back on top
22. Long overdue
23. Back pedal
24. Water under the bridge
25. Leaning over

Answers to Fact or Fancy
From page 99

1. *I* We're inferring Wallace is a man—Wallace could be a woman.
2. *I* Wallace was scheduled for a meeting in Mr. Johnson's office—but not necessarily with Mr. Johnson.
3. *F* Wallace *was* scheduled for an 11 o'clock meeting.
4. *I* The story says only that the incident occurred *on the way* to Johnson's office—but it could have happened anywhere, like in Wallace's own home.
5. *I* We don't know whether Wallace was taken to the hospital for an injection or whether he or she drove.
6. *I* No one that *Johnson* talked to seemed to know about Wallace—but that doesn't mean some other person didn't.
7. *I* We don't *know* whether Johnson called the wrong hospital or not. We're only guessing.

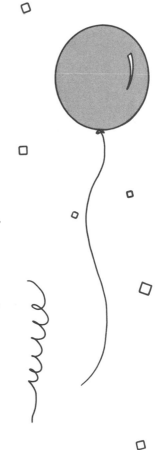

Answers to Planet Earth
From page 101

1. The Red Sea
2. Capetown, Pretoria, Johannesburg, Durban, Port Elizabeth
3. In the Irish Sea, between England and Ireland
4. Singapore
5. In the Tasman Sea, due south of Melbourne
6. Greece
7. France and the UK
8. Sri Lanka
9. Sofia
10. Beijing
11. Haiti and the Dominican Republic
12. Kabul
13. The northernmost portion of Scandinavia, inhabited by the Lapps
14. Kuala Lumpur
15. The latitudes (23.5 degrees) defining the Torrid Zone (as distance from the Temperate and Frigid Zones). The Tropic of Cancer is in the Northern Hemisphere.
16. Bangladesh (formerly East Pakistan)
17. Kampuchea
18. The Caspian Sea
19. The Nile (less than 100 miles longer than the Missouri-Mississippi and the Amazon)
20. In Central America, east of Guatemala and south of Yucatan, Mexico
21. Kilimanjaro (19,321 feet)

Answers to Hidden Word Puzzle
From page 133

```
S T E I H L M E X T E B N Q M
E X M A S T B A B Y Y G U U C
T O N S M O N F U N A I S R A
Y B O T T L E M N S L F T E P
A V P R E G N A N T B T A A O
D T O O E A R N Y K O S N T W
H F A L T G I R L I Y U Q T D
T G E L H B D I A P E R O U E
R B M E I T M P C N R M Y S R
I D O R N P A L S R Y C O B L
B A T H G O B O E S Y D E M I
W G H X T I N H S N N I M A B
J N E A R A T T L E Q T S O E
S O R C R A W L O U D U U D A
P R Y F A M I L Y S H O W E R
```

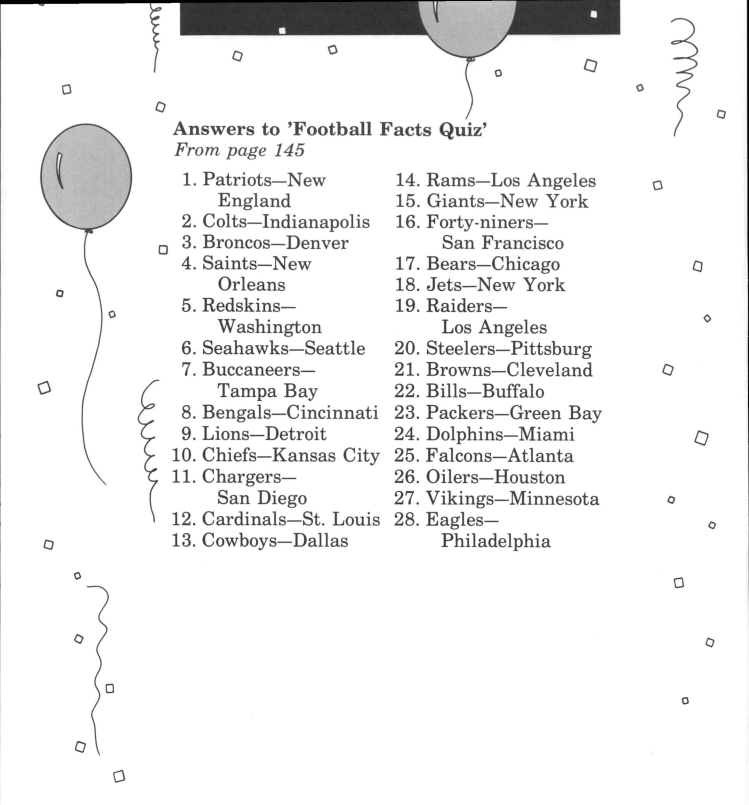

Answers to 'Football Facts Quiz'
From page 145

1. Patriots—New England
2. Colts—Indianapolis
3. Broncos—Denver
4. Saints—New Orleans
5. Redskins—Washington
6. Seahawks—Seattle
7. Buccaneers—Tampa Bay
8. Bengals—Cincinnati
9. Lions—Detroit
10. Chiefs—Kansas City
11. Chargers—San Diego
12. Cardinals—St. Louis
13. Cowboys—Dallas
14. Rams—Los Angeles
15. Giants—New York
16. Forty-niners—San Francisco
17. Bears—Chicago
18. Jets—New York
19. Raiders—Los Angeles
20. Steelers—Pittsburg
21. Browns—Cleveland
22. Bills—Buffalo
23. Packers—Green Bay
24. Dolphins—Miami
25. Falcons—Atlanta
26. Oilers—Houston
27. Vikings—Minnesota
28. Eagles—Philadelphia

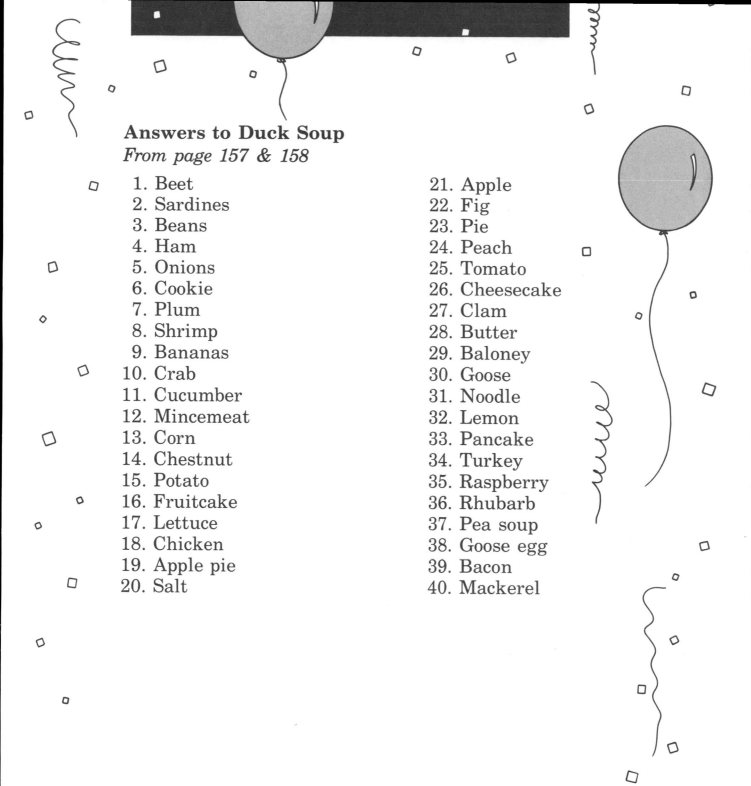

Answers to Duck Soup
From page 157 & 158

1. Beet
2. Sardines
3. Beans
4. Ham
5. Onions
6. Cookie
7. Plum
8. Shrimp
9. Bananas
10. Crab
11. Cucumber
12. Mincemeat
13. Corn
14. Chestnut
15. Potato
16. Fruitcake
17. Lettuce
18. Chicken
19. Apple pie
20. Salt

21. Apple
22. Fig
23. Pie
24. Peach
25. Tomato
26. Cheesecake
27. Clam
28. Butter
29. Baloney
30. Goose
31. Noodle
32. Lemon
33. Pancake
34. Turkey
35. Raspberry
36. Rhubarb
37. Pea soup
38. Goose egg
39. Bacon
40. Mackerel

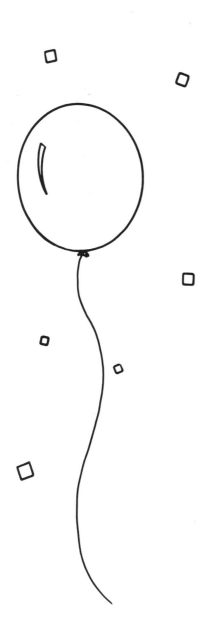